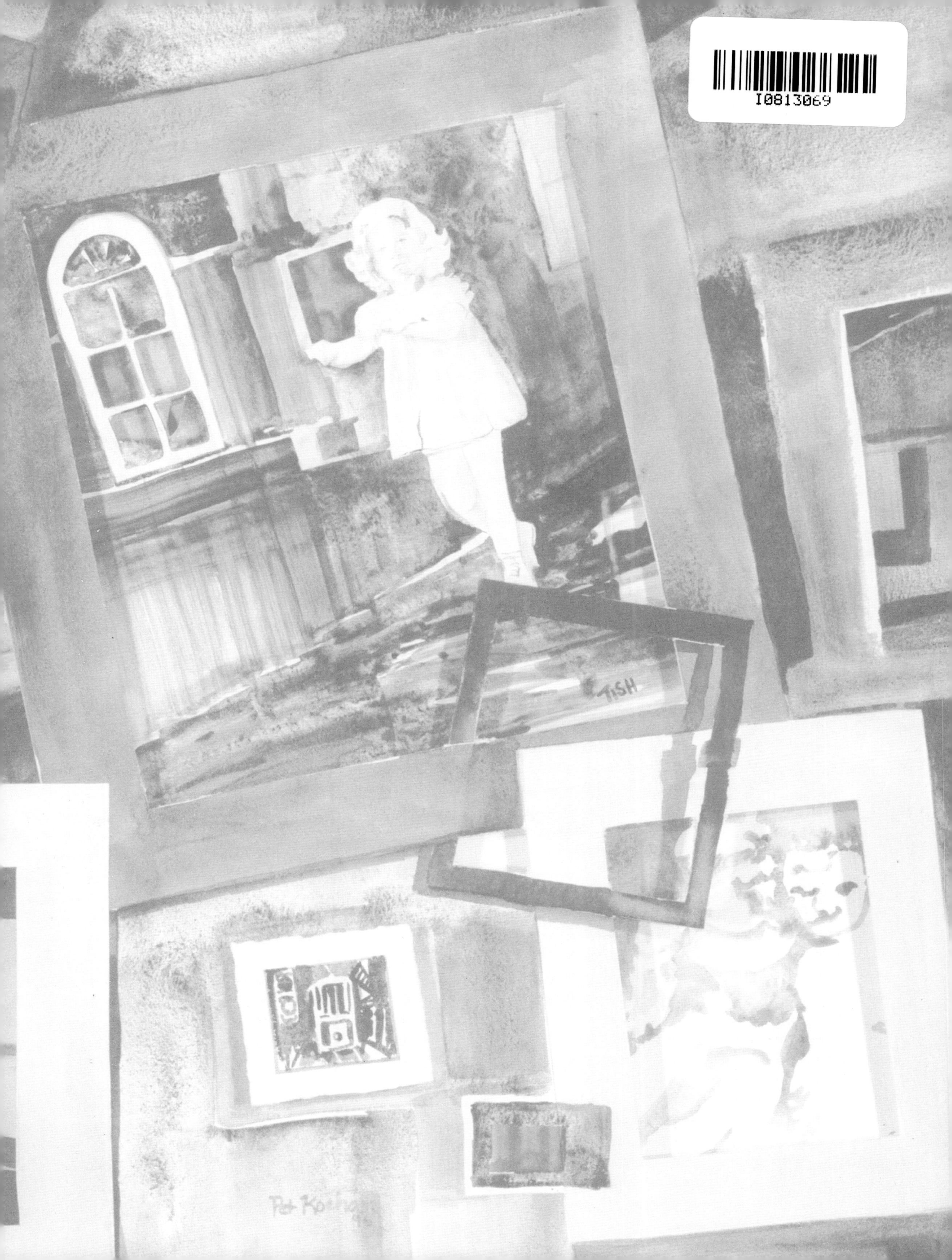
TISH

Once upon a Time in Dallas

Once upon a Time in Dallas

Through the Artist's Eyes

Pat Wheelis Kochan

Once upon a Time in Dallas: Through the Artist's Eyes

Manufactured in Singapore.

For information, please contact:
Brown Books Publishing Group
16200 North Dallas Parkway, Suite 170
Dallas, Texas 75248
www.brownbooks.com
972-381-0009

ISBN 1-933285-00-1
LCCN 2005920862
2 3 4 5 6 7 8 9 10

To My Family

This book is dedicated to my husband, John, who has supported me in my pursuit of art and assisted me in so many ways; to my son, Curt, who courageously taught me to use the computer; to my daughter, Christy, who generously put my work on the Web; to my daughter-in-law, Laura, for her encouragement; to my son-in-law, Mark, who edited this book; and to the memory of my parents, Bill and Elsie, who continually encouraged me to pursue my dreams of being an artist.

I hope that this book will be a legacy to my granddaughters, Camaryn, Sarah, and Olivia, and to future grandchildren.

I would like to express my appreciation to Beatrice Hicks for giving me the push I needed and for helping me write and publish this book.

Contents

Introduction

From one commissioned painting evolved this pictorial history of Dallas from the 1950s through the final decade of the twentieth century. The artist is a woman, Pat Wheelis Kochan, a native of Dallas, whose love for this city is nurtured by her fond childhood memories of a time when people went "downtown" for shopping, doctors' appointments, dance classes, and entertainment, just to name a few. Included in this series are nostalgic paintings of buildings that were a major influence on the peoples of Dallas. Some of the buildings no longer exist. Some have been saved, thanks to preservationists. Some still are in use today, and others stand vacant.

Two outstanding qualities of Pat Wheelis Kochan are tenacity and fairness, as evidenced by her series of paintings of downtown Dallas. Her childhood and family life played an important part in how she perceived her surroundings and greatly influenced what she painted.

Kochan started her downtown Dallas series as a commissioned work for a client who wanted a painting of the Dallas Tortilla Factory in Little Mexico, to preserve its memory before the building was torn down. The series grew as she captured what was meaningful and nostalgic to her.

I have learned to understand Dallas from Kochan's perspective. Her father was a salesman who entertained clients in the finest restaurants in the city. Often he would include his wife and daughter at these business dinners. Kochan grew up in an era when it was safe for a small child to ride the streetcar, unassisted by an adult, as she often did to get from her home in Oak Cliff to dance class or tumbling class in downtown Dallas. As a young girl, Kochan viewed the buildings and the ornate sculptures with fascination and wonder. Her painting of the little girl looking up at the Magnolia building captures the grandness of the edifice. Her flying red horse also charms every child and sparks the memories we all have of seeing Dallas for the first time from a distance with Pegasus as the beacon.

Kochan also is not afraid to use artistic license in painting with the colors she likes, adding drama and perspective, or painting people in front of buildings that exist in her memory as a compilation of known structures and sculptures.

Kochan says that she feels she has a responsibility to report Dallas' roots as she knows them and to do it with mystery and beautiful color. I like her philosophy: "Paint who you are," she says. "I am a city girl, so I paint the city and its people."

I think you, too, will be enriched by this artist's portrayal of buildings, color, and reminiscences of the past fifty years. Perhaps it will spark some heartwarming memories of your own.

—Beatrice Hicks

Artist's Statement

My paintings are about downtown Dallas, the old and the new. Attitudes about downtown must change if we are to save the heritage of our wonderful city. Growing up in Oak Cliff, Oak Lawn, and North Dallas, I thought of Dallas as a little New York City. When you went to town shopping, to the movies, or to eat at wonderful restaurants, you always saw people you knew. There were so many people on the streets at night that you were never afraid of crime. The streetcar took us back and forth between Oak Cliff or Oak Lawn and downtown.

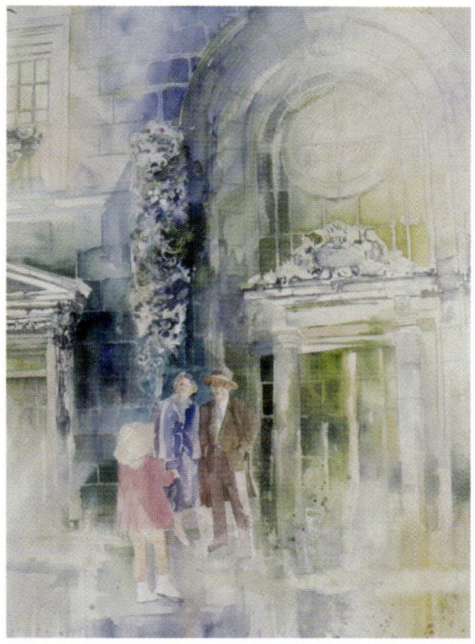

Dance classes with Virginia Self Dance Studio were downtown on Saturday mornings. Once a month there was a parade, and we would watch it from the open windows during class (there was no air conditioning at that time). At seven years old, I would go downtown by myself via streetcar for tumbling lessons at the Dallas Athletic Club on St. Paul Street. My dad, who worked at the Tower Petroleum Building on Elm Street, would take me home after work. Doctors and dentists were in the Medical Arts Building, now gone from the skyline. Those were special times and special memories: the ice show at the Adolphus, Dad's offices in the Magnolia Building and the Tower Petroleum Building, shopping with Mom at H. L. Green Co. and Neiman Marcus, seeing a movie, and riding the streetcar home (we had only one car then).

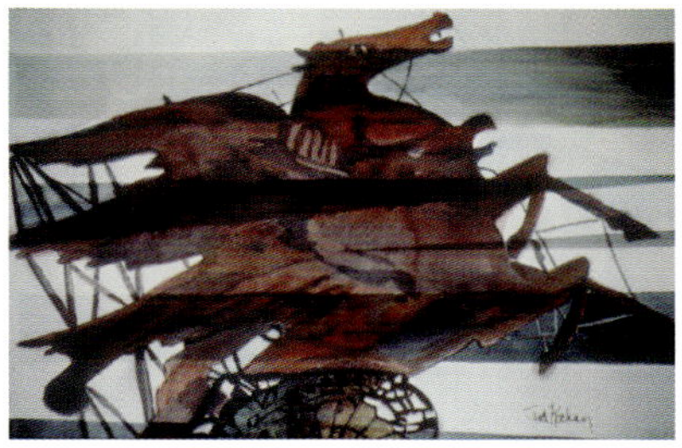

Looking up at the big buildings and bright lights was exciting to me. That is why I paint the buildings from downtown Dallas. They are part of my roots, pieces of Dallas' history. We must preserve as much of the past as possible in order to direct the future for our city. Many old Dallas buildings have been demolished, but I have sketches, I have photos, and I have memories that I can paint. Collectors buy them to preserve their memories, too. I will add to this series of paintings of downtown Dallas as change alters the skyline, because these places that have shaped lives and evoked memories must live on, if only through my artwork.

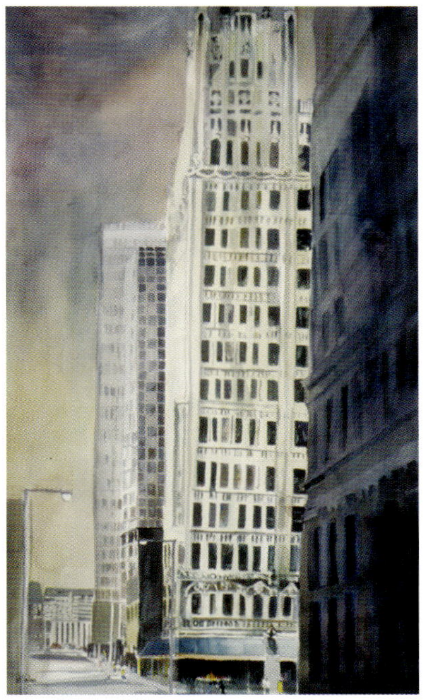

I would hope that these paintings affirm to each viewer the fact that Dallas is a special city.

—Pat Wheelis Kochan

Biography

Pat Wheelis Kochan is a professional artist from Dallas, Texas. She studied art and design at the University of Colorado and has worked in watermedia, acrylic, oil and mixed media. She continued her art study with many nationally known teachers. She has taught art at her studio, Artisan's Studio-Gallery, for several years and gives workshops for art organizations. She is a writer, lecturer, juror, and demonstrator for art groups.

Kochan is well known in the Dallas area for her series of paintings of old downtown Dallas. Many hang in offices and homes in Dallas and other cities in the United States. She was recognized for her series by "Dallas Proud" of the Office of Cultural Affairs in the mayor's office. Kochan's series of abstract paintings has also won her recognition in competitions. Her paintings have been in major exhibitions throughout the United States, such as National Watercolor Society; Rocky Mountain National Watermedia in Colorado; Adirondacks National Exhibition of American Watercolor, New York; Watercolor USA 2004, Springfield Missouri Art Museum; Georgia National Watercolor; Oklahoma National Watercolor; Italian Exhibition for Southwestern Watercolor Society in Milan, Italy; and Western Federation of Watercolor Societies, Albuquerque Museum, to name a few. Her paintings have won many awards. In 1995 and 1997, she was commissioned to create large-scale acrylic landscape paintings on canvas for the lobbies of a large office building. In 2001, she was commissioned by the city to produce a work for the Dallas Soars Pegasus project.

As a founding member of ART FOCUS XC, Kochan has exhibited her work at JC Penney Corporate Headquarters, Collin County Community College, Longview Art Museum, Fort Worth Health Science Center Atrium Gallery, Rockport Center for the Arts, and Corpus Christi Art Center. Kochan has been awarded Signature Status of the Southwestern Watercolor Society, Texas Visual Arts Association, Texas Watercolor Society, and National Acrylic Painters' Association UK. She has received the prestigious Purple Sage Society Pin in Texas Watercolor Society for her records of awards in watercolor societies. She served on the board of directors and was the "Spotlight Editor" of the Scene for Southwestern Watercolor Society. Kochan served on the board of directors as show chairman of the Texas Visual Arts Association Signature Group and has served as delegate-at-large for the Texas Watercolor Society in San Antonio, Texas. Kochan served each year as juror for the Dallas Business for the Arts "On My Own Time" competition.

Kochan's work has been featured in *Southwest Art* magazine, November 1996; *American Artist* Publication's Watercolor, 1999; *Texas Watercolor Fifty Years of Excellence,* 1999; Rockport's Publisher's *Best of Watercolor,* 1998; The *Collected Best of Watercolor,* 2002; and the *Dallas Morning News,* the *Fort Worth Star-Telegram* and the *Rocky Mountain News.* Kochan and the studio she shares with three other artists was featured in the *American Artist Magazine* in August 1999; and in *Splash 7* (Northlight Publisher's) in 2002. David Flick of the *Dallas Morning News* published an article about Kochan and her downtown Dallas series in his column "About Downtown" in 2004.

Windows of My Soul Series: Child's Viewpoint

watercolor
53x33

When I was a little girl, I would look up at this tall, slender building with all of its ornate decoration in amazement. I think the A. Harris Department Store was in this building.

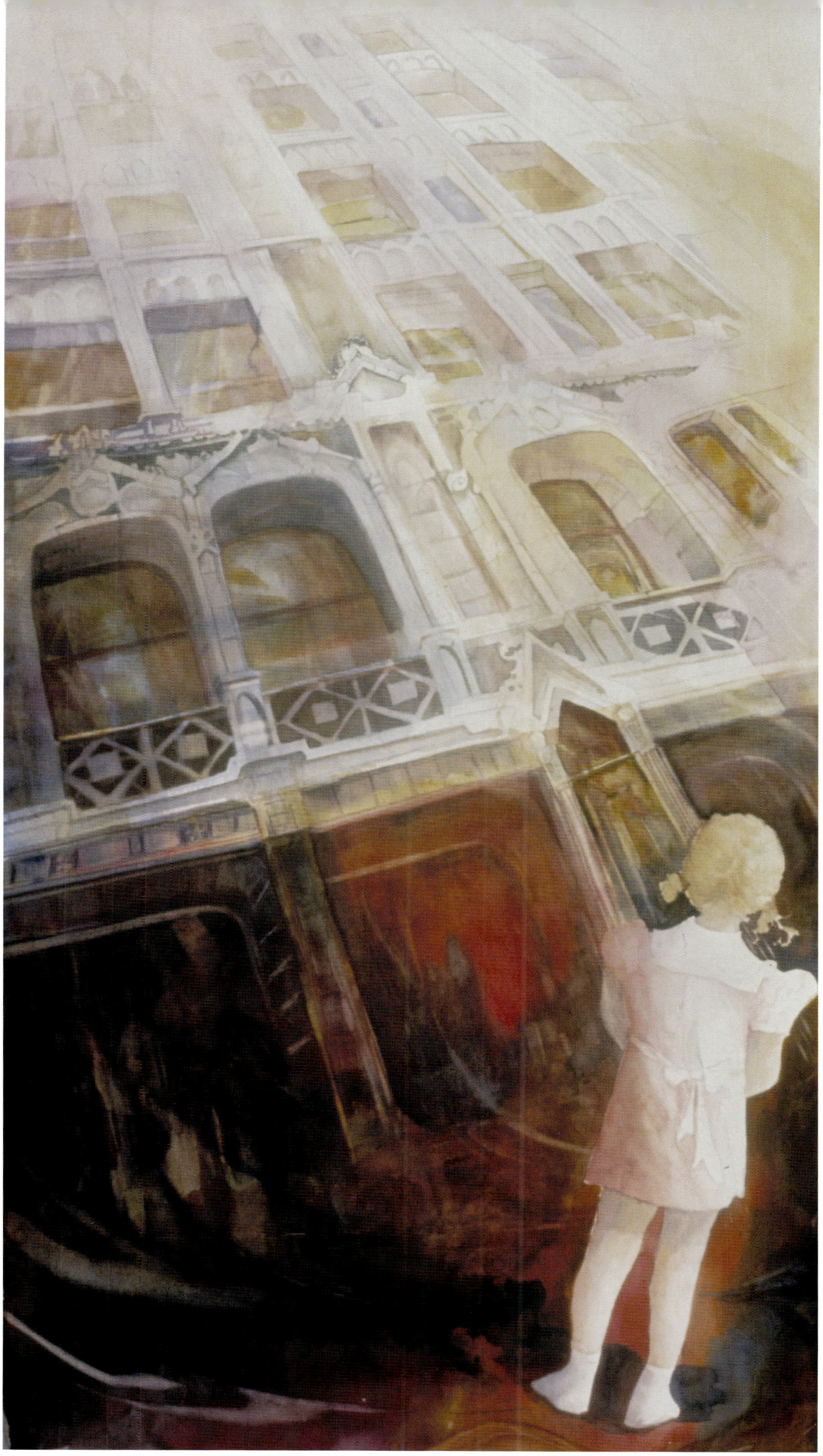

Kirby Building

watercolor
43x26

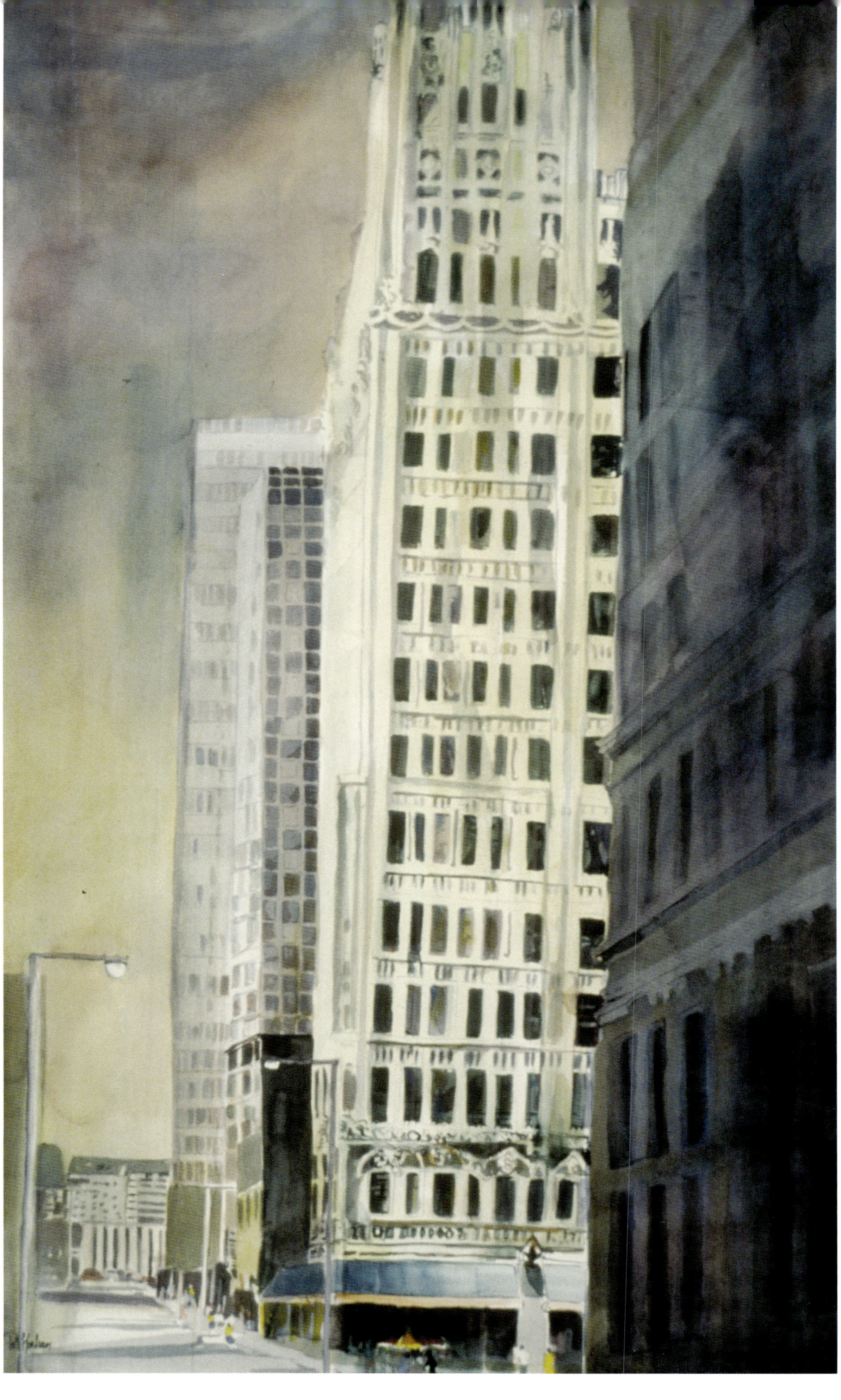

Windows of My Soul Series: Open Windows

watercolor collage
28x34

In this painting, I was interested in giving a three-dimensional look, so I collaged small paintings of the Adolphus Hotel, Magnolia Building, a streetcar and me as a child, all symbolic of my years growing up in Dallas.

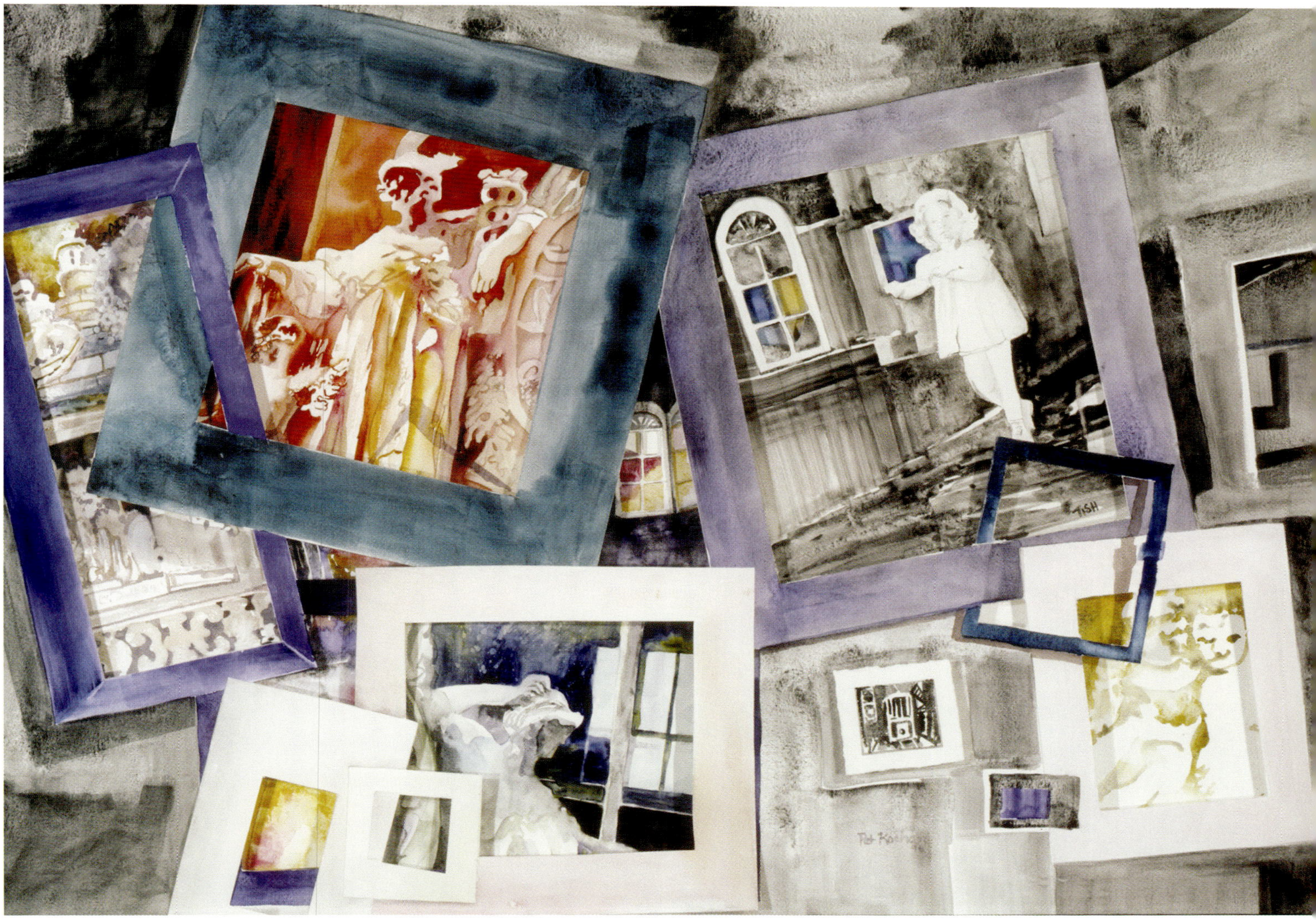

Ghosts of Dallas

watercolor
36x30

This painting is very personal, full of symbolism. The shape of a cross anchors the piece. At the top of the cross are images from the Adolphus Hotel that represent a man and woman, my mom and dad, who introduced me to Dallas. Movie marquees, the streetcar (from the Elm Street Close-up painting), and my dad and mom entertaining customers at a fine hotel are represented.

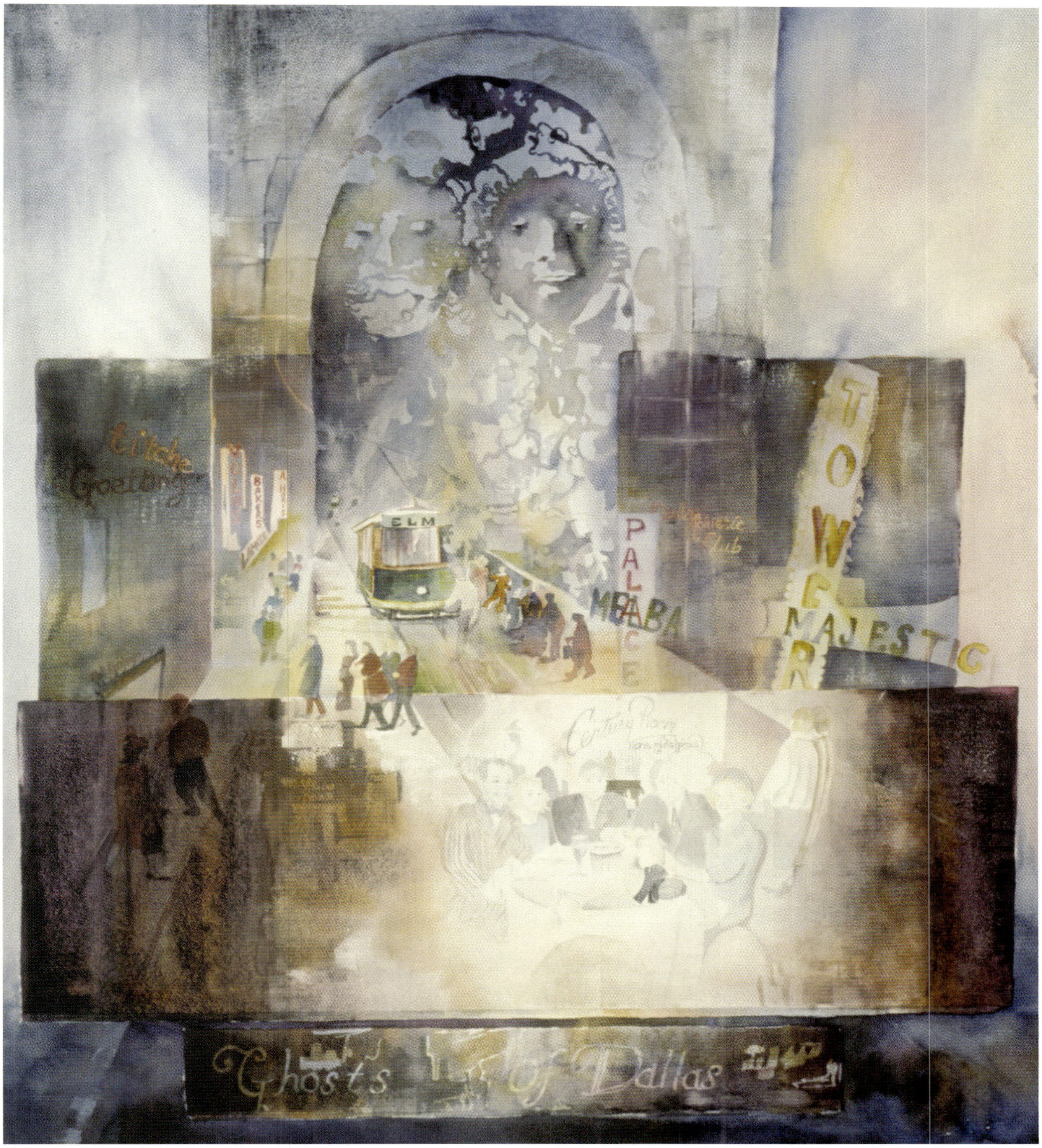
Titche
Goettinger
ELM
PALACE
TOWER
MAJESTIC
Ghosts of Dallas

Lady in Red

watercolor
38x52

Although many of these paintings depict buildings both historical and ornate, they are really significant of a period and the essence of a lifetime of people who formed a past and planted seeds for the future. The Lady in Red is my mother, the wife of a salesman. She often accompanied her husband during evenings at lavish hotel dining rooms, where he would entertain customers. This evening happened to be at the Baker Hotel.

Her hat was a great part of being a lady in those days. Women rarely went anywhere in public without wearing one. The hat established a mood. Back then if a lady became unsettled or depressed over everyday boredom, she could lift her spirits again by simply buying a new hat. And of course the little handbag and gloves were very necessary accessories for the properly attired.

Downtown was dressy; the mood was classy and fun. As for the two men in the painting, the one on the right represents my dad, the “Mr. Personality” of the group, always laughing and making people feel good. He is discussing the lovely lady with his friend and customer. From the day my parents were married, it was obvious that Dad adored his wife, and she knew it. The customer here, if memory serves, was Mr. Martin with Great Western Foods in Fort Worth. The sculptural background of figures motif is from the Baker Hotel.

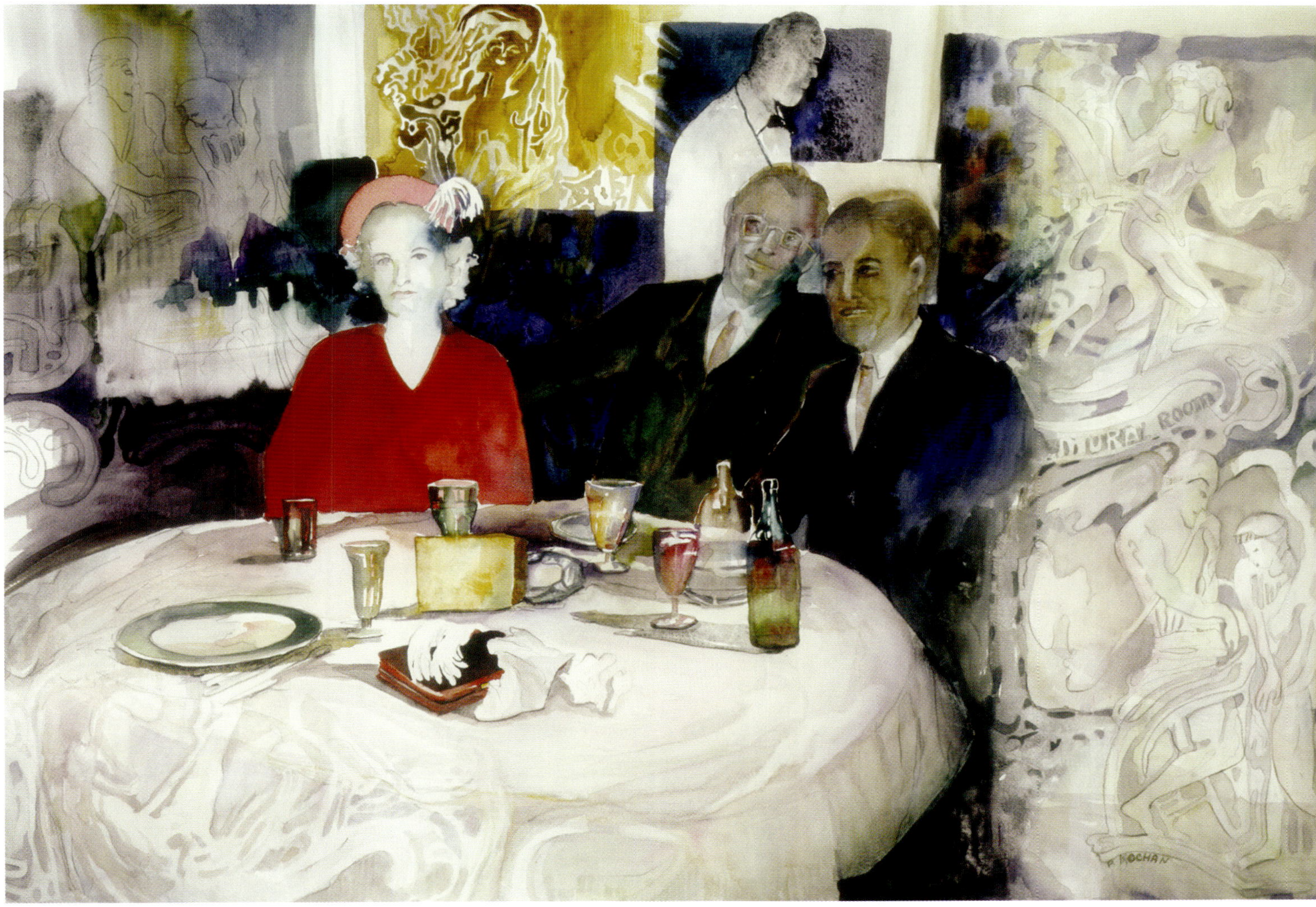
MURAL Room

Flying Red Horse

watercolor
28x34

My dad worked for the Continental Can Company. His first office was in the Magnolia Building with the flying red horse on top. The Pegasus was the tallest icon in the city and was a landmark for everyone for miles around. Through my eyes as a child, it was so exciting to see the revolving horse perched on top of the towering building. Many of my paintings have been inspired by this magnificent sculpture.

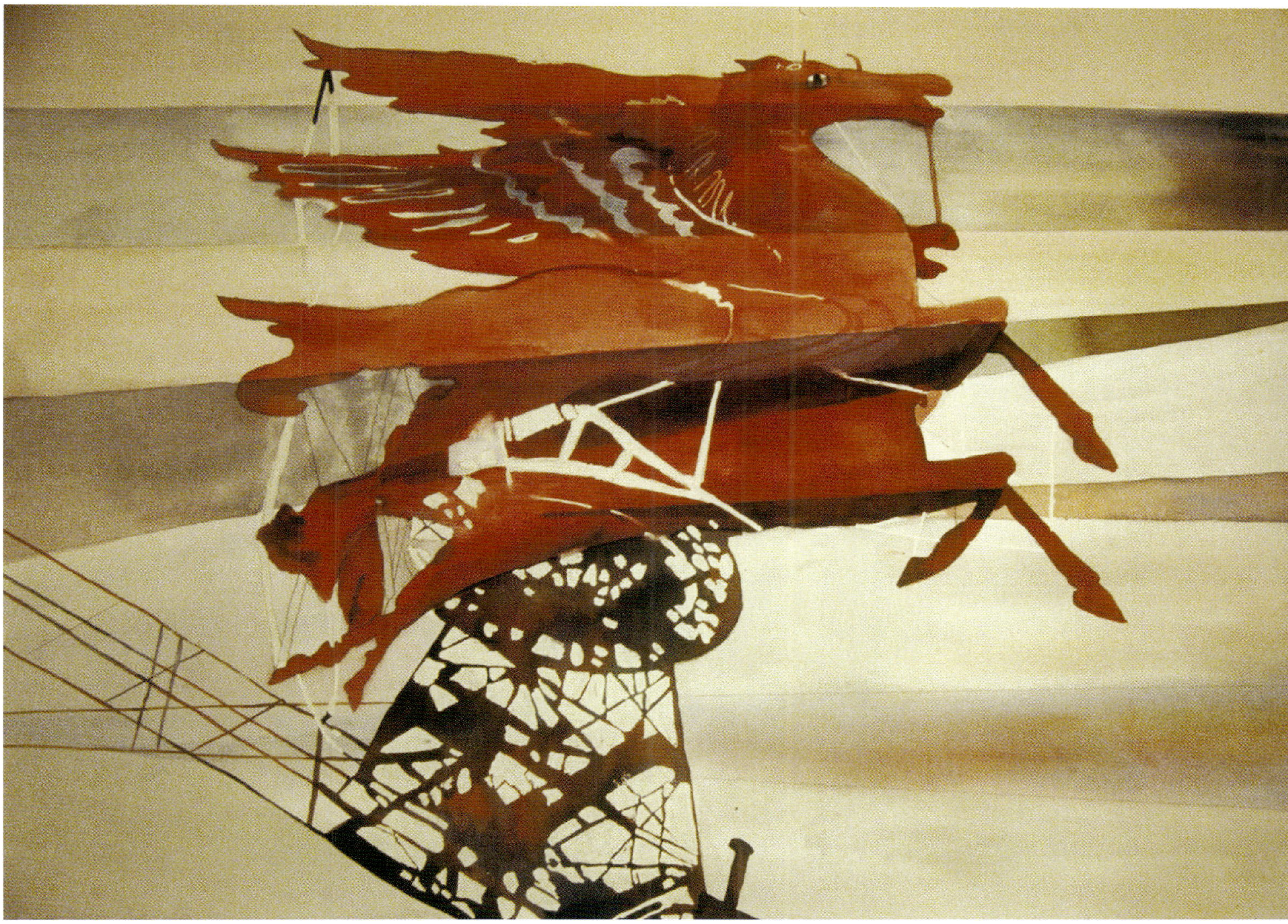

Magnolia Building 1

watercolor
44x38

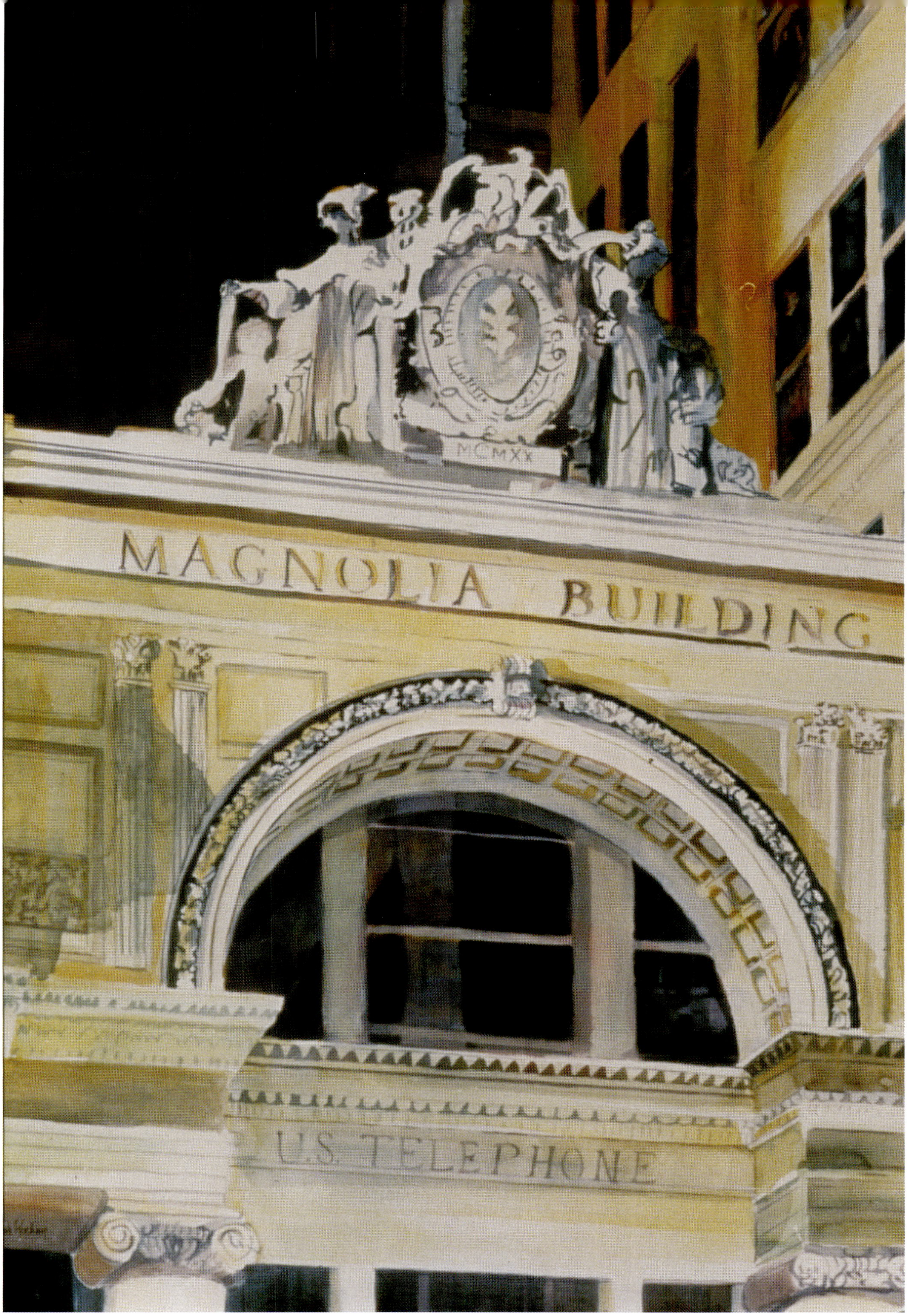
MCMXX
MAGNOLIA BUILDING
U.S. TELEPHONE

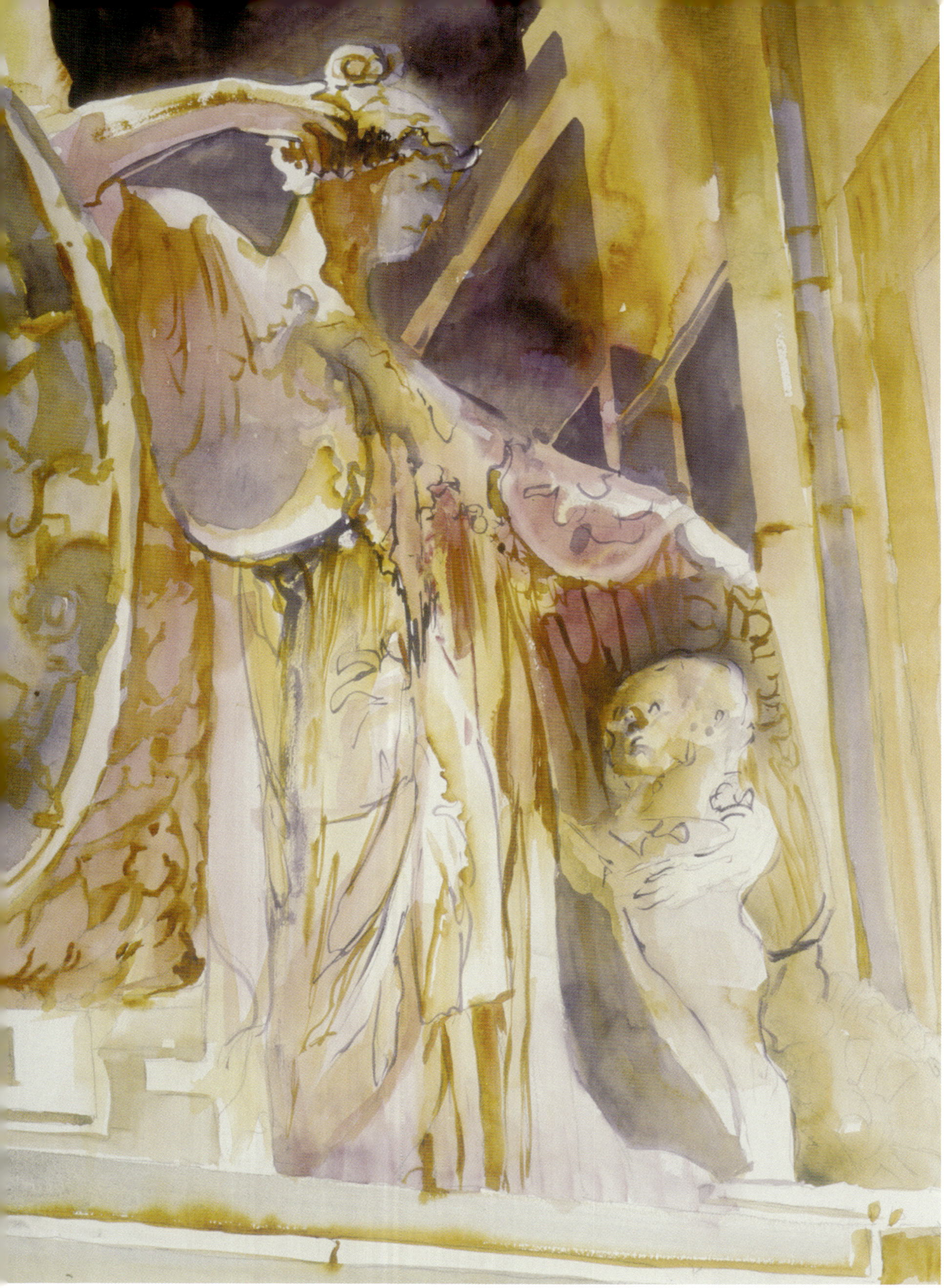

Magnolia Sculpture I

watercolor
36x28

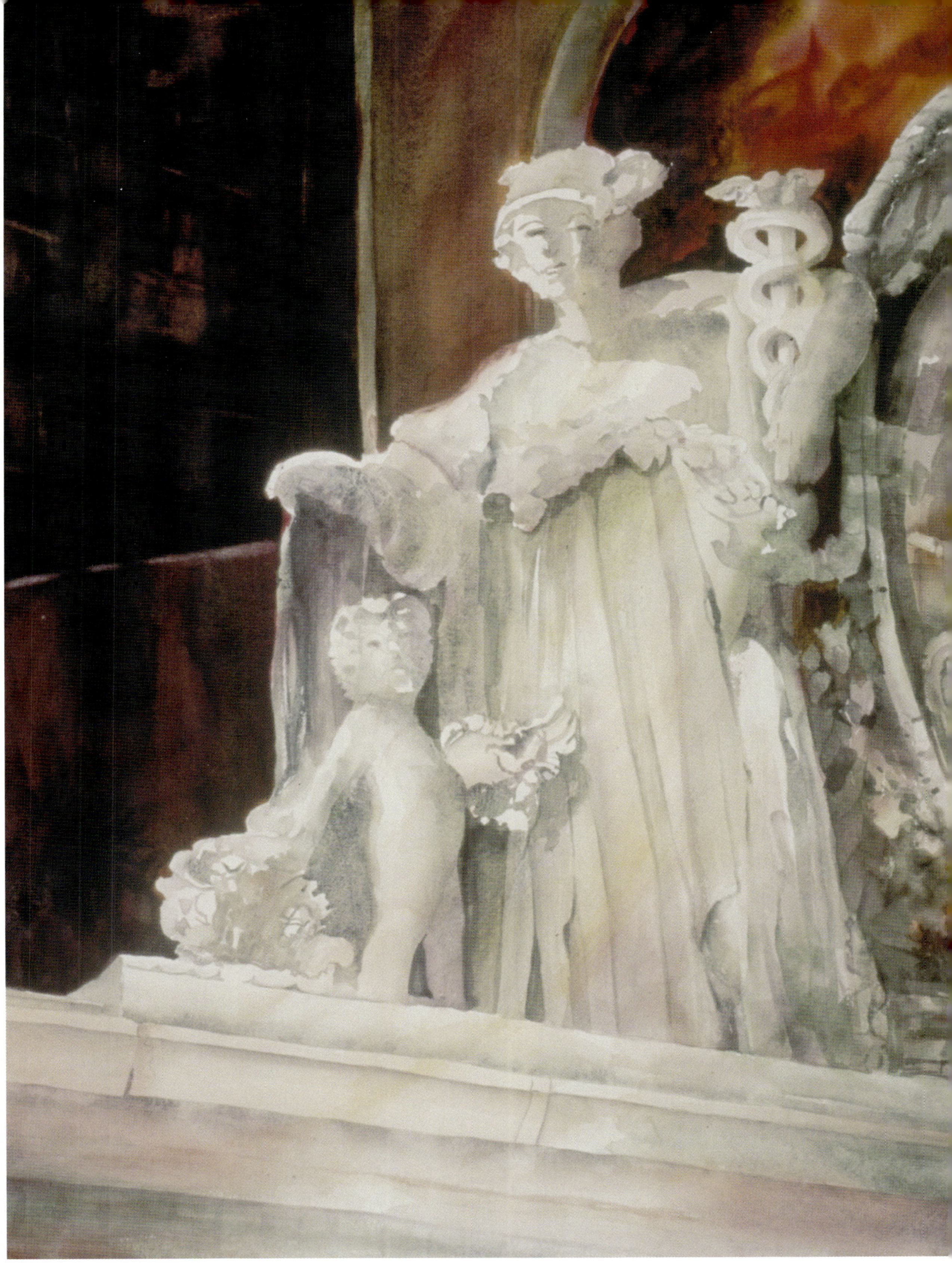

Magnolia Sculpture II

watercolor
36x28

Dallas Sculptures

watercolor
49x41

This painting was completed in 1995 and is a montage of several pieces I created for the downtown Dallas series. As the downtown area has made a comeback, more emphasis has been placed on preserving the past. Some of the buildings I have captured in this painting include the Kirby Building, in the upper left corner; the Adolphus Hotel with its cherubs and sculptures on either side, the window on the left and the rail at the bottom; and the Magnolia Building, represented by the sculptures of the four figures around the eagle/oval.

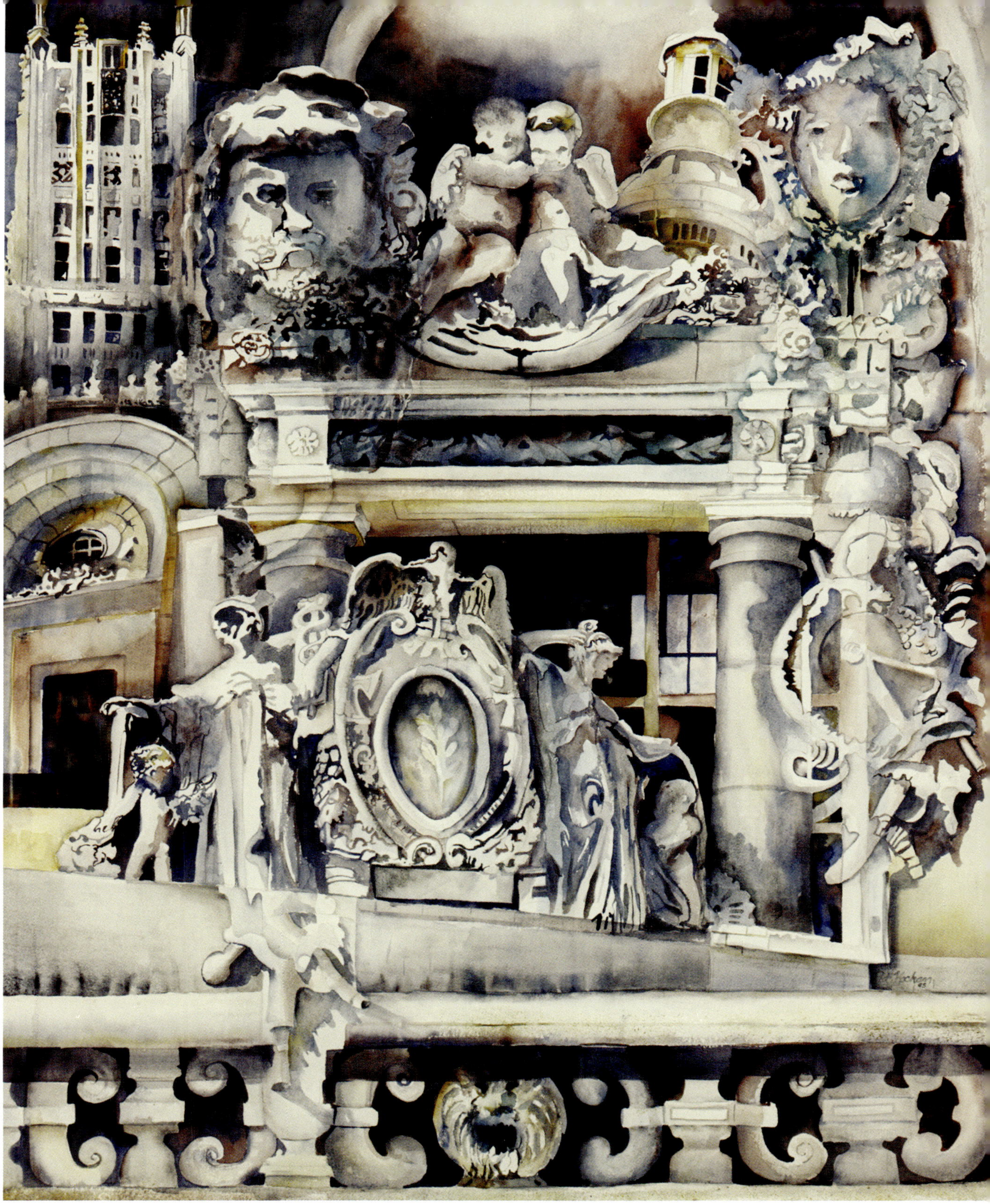

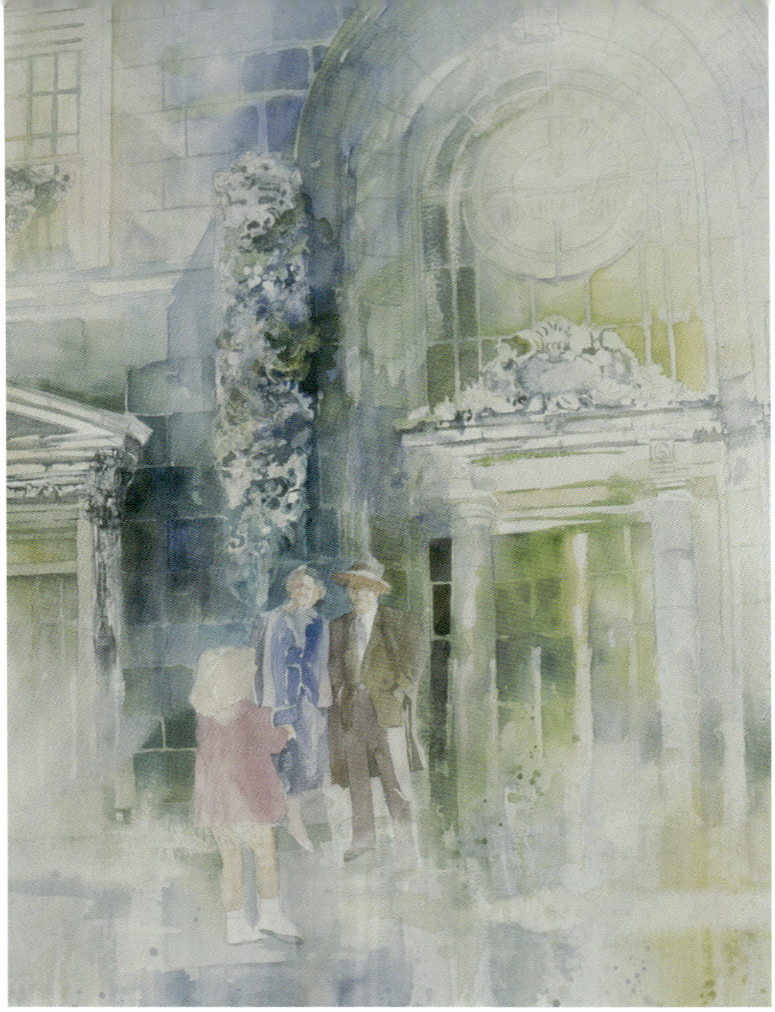

Family at the Adolphus

watercolor
30x22

The Baker Hotel

In 1997, I began a series of paintings from photos that my parents had taken during dinners in hotels, such as the Adolphus and the Baker. In this painting, the window looking out at the skyline and the left corner motif in the background represent the Baker Hotel. Notice the black bag and white gloves on the table; my mom always carried them in the '40s and '50s.

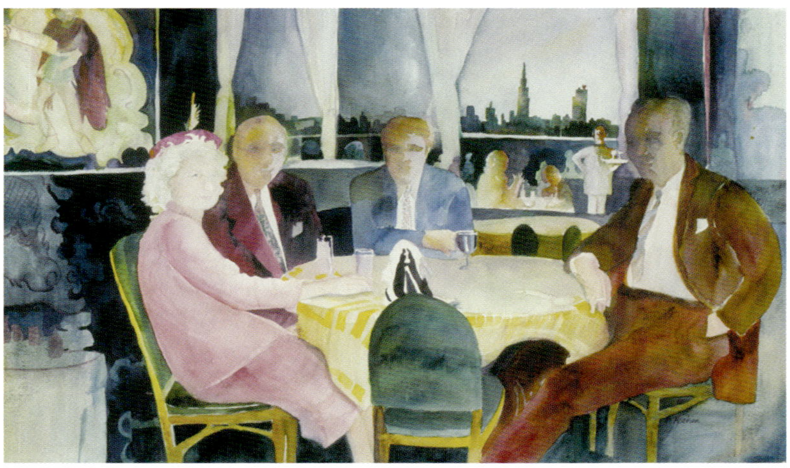

Elsie in Pink

watercolor
24x40

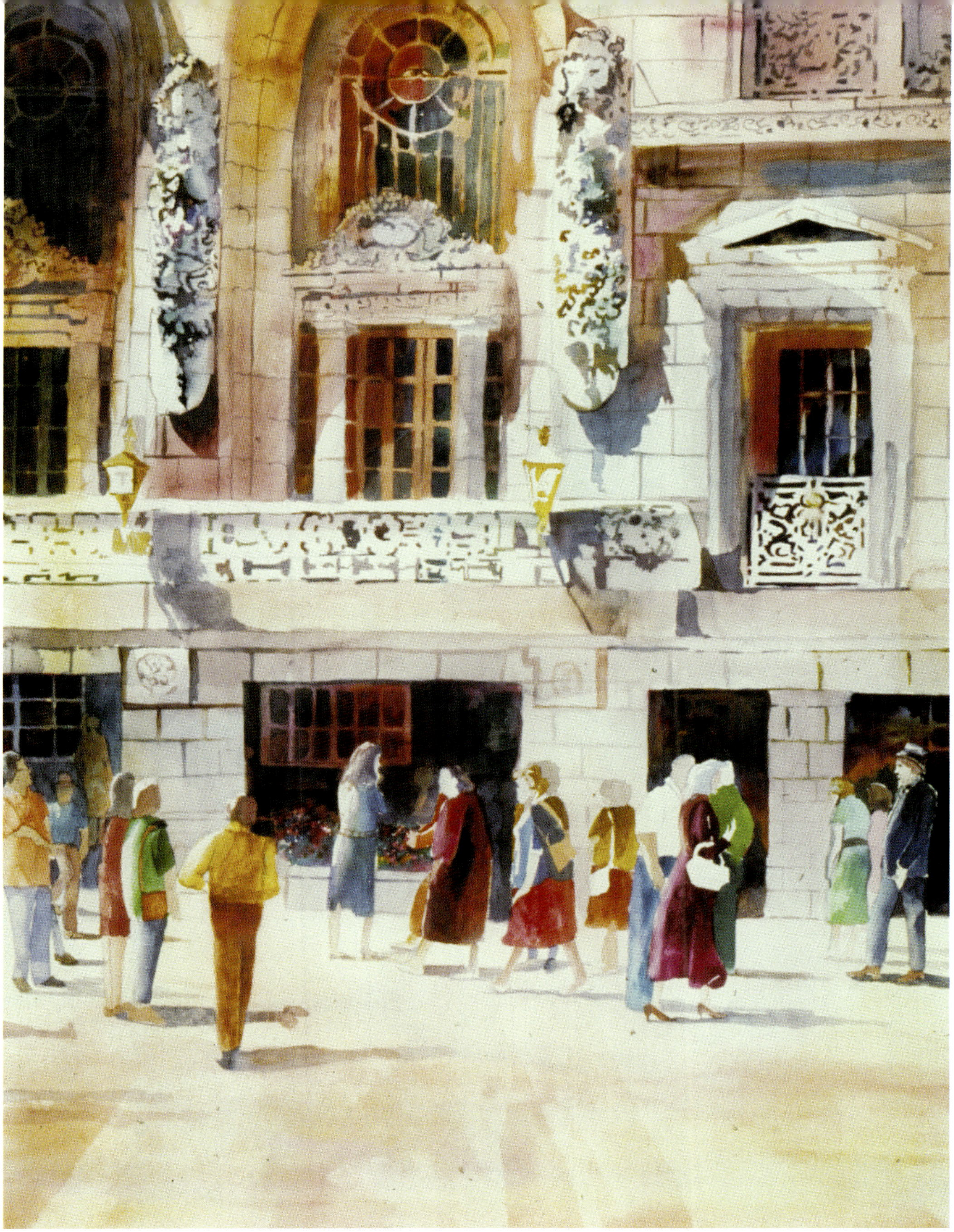

Adolphus #14

watercolor
30x22

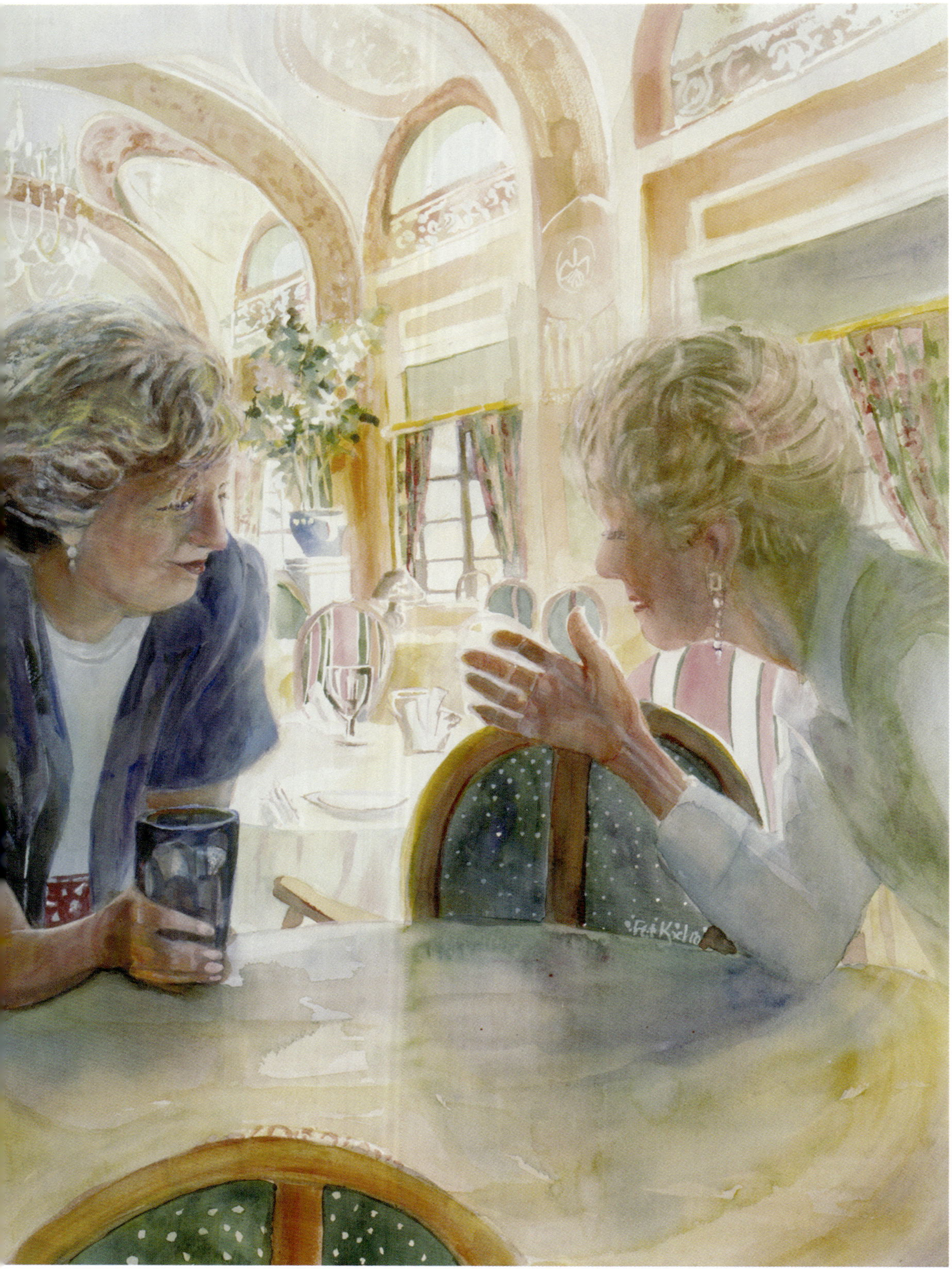

Conversation in the French Room

watercolor
22x30

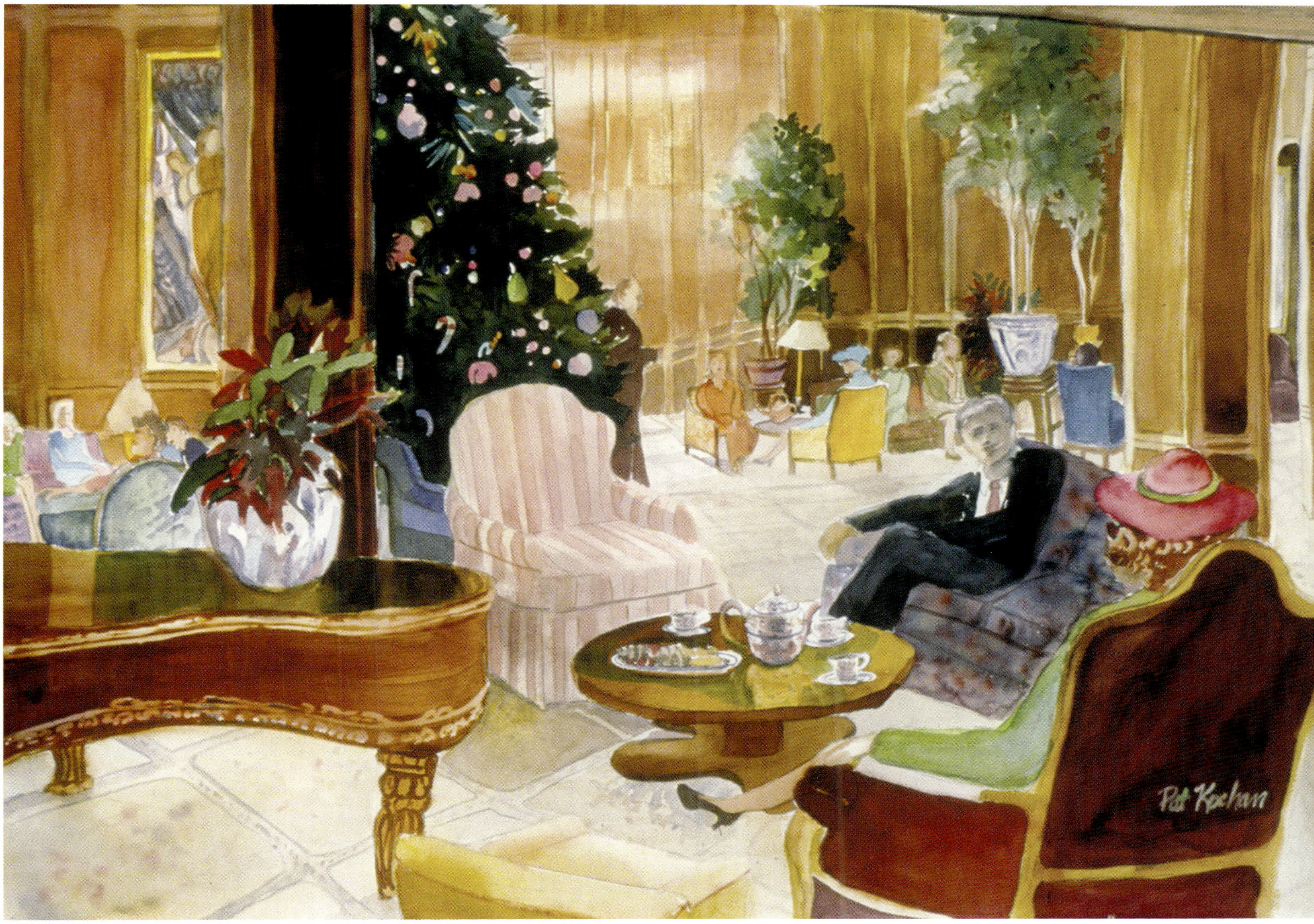

Tea Time at the Adolphus

watercolor
22x30

Adolphus Parade #2

watercolor
22x30

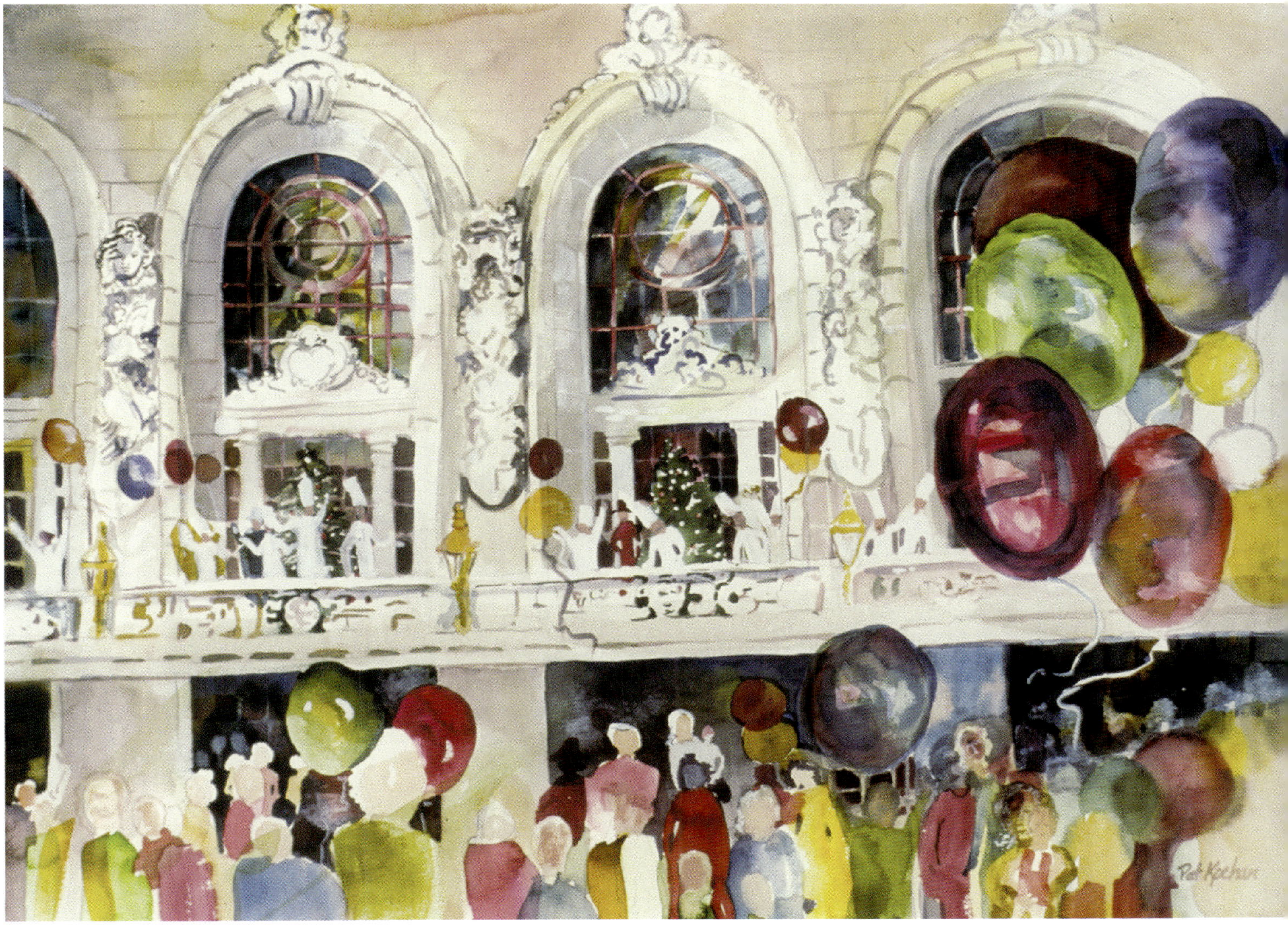

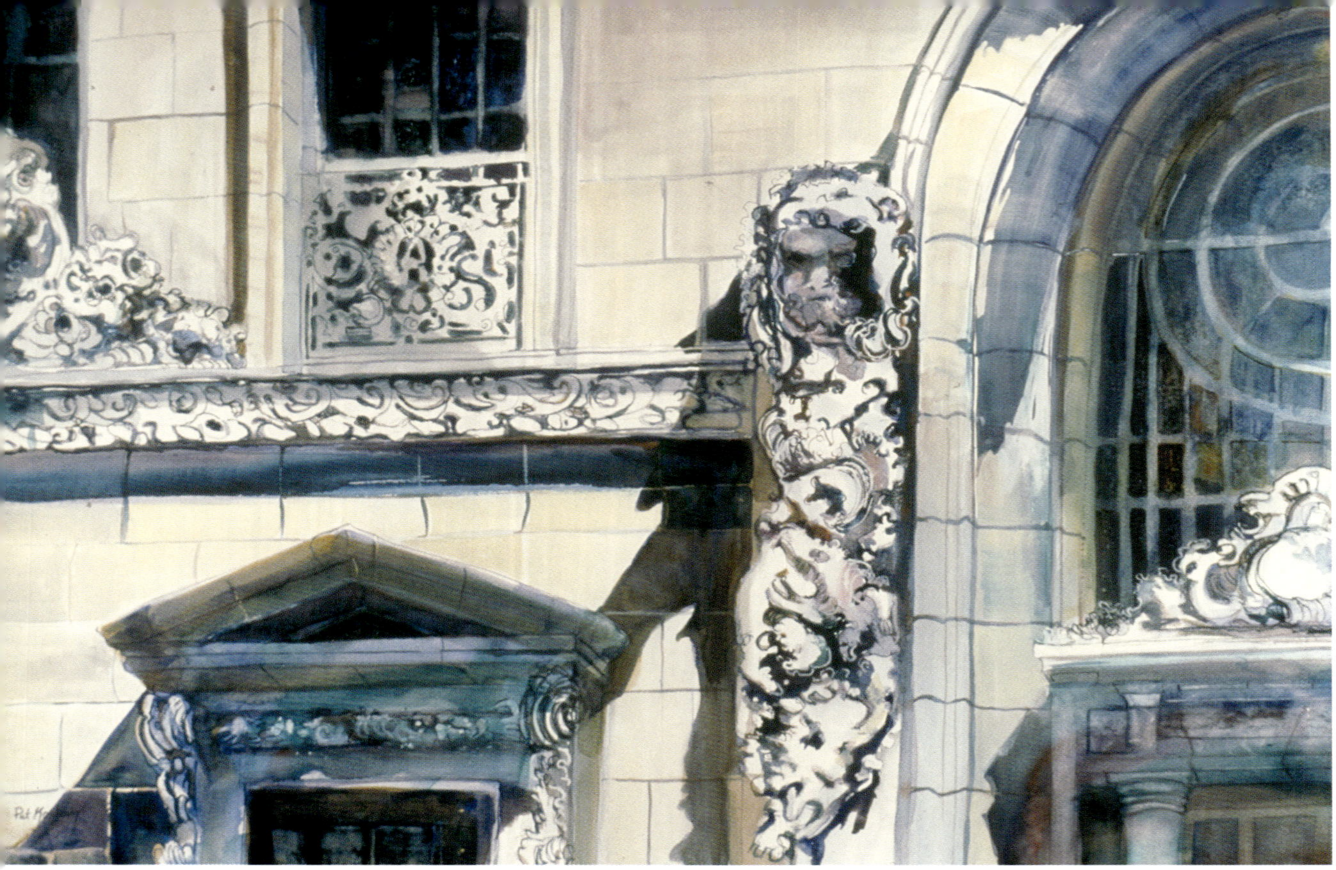

Adolphus Series #8

watercolor
30x40

The Adolphus Hotel

Since my dad often entertained customers for dinner, he went to the finest restaurants in Dallas and Fort Worth. I frequently accompanied my parents because babysitters were not easy to come by, and my parents felt I needed to learn the "social graces." We often went to the Century Room of the Adolphus Hotel for dinner, an ice show, and dancing. It was wonderful, and I loved the ice skating show and, of course, dancing on my daddy's toes. I have painted this magnificent building many times, so often perhaps that the beautiful shapes of its ornamentation seem to appear in many of my paintings of other subjects. They have become second nature in my subconscious. These European sculptures on the building give Dallas a taste of the Old World without leaving the city.

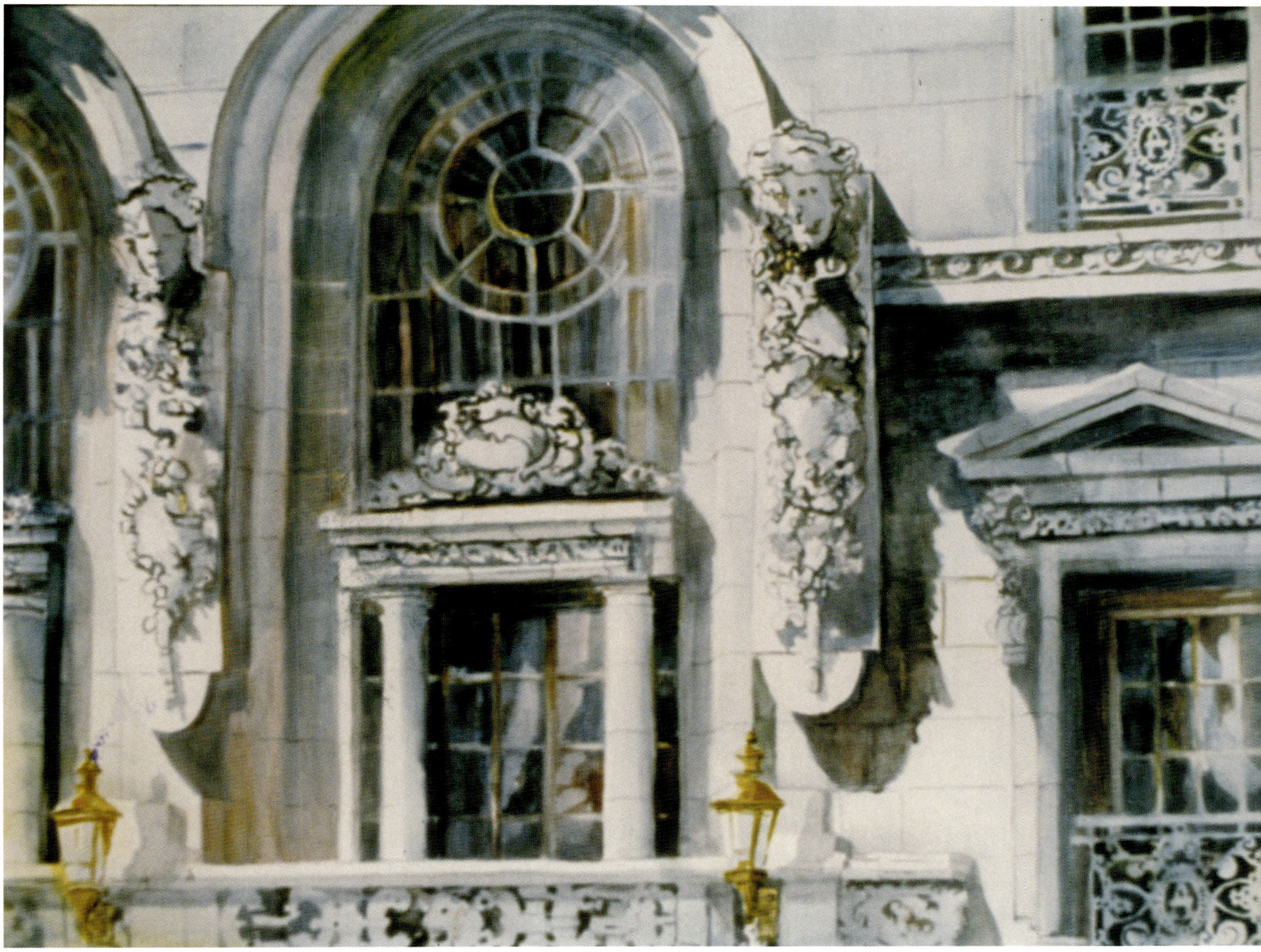

Adolphus Series #7

watercolor
22x30

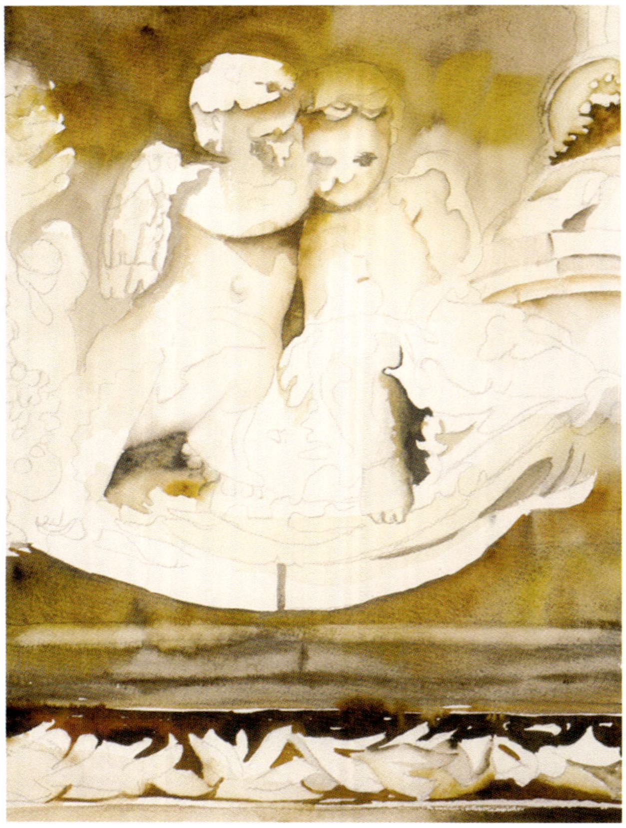

Adolphus Cherubs

watercolor
15x11

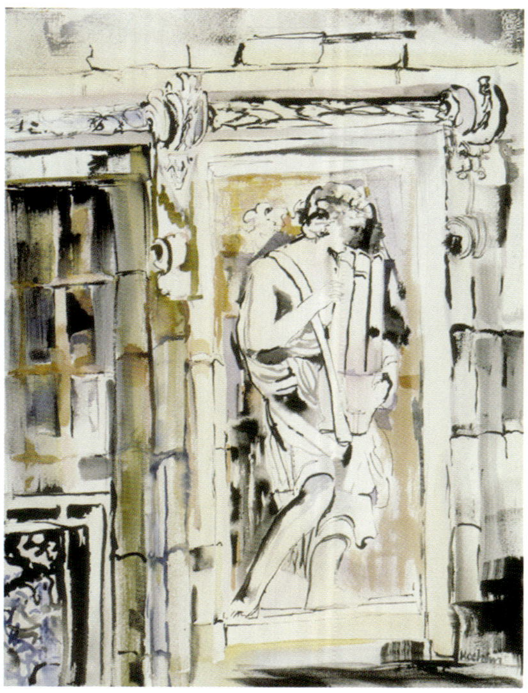

Adolphus Sculpture I

watercolor
30x22

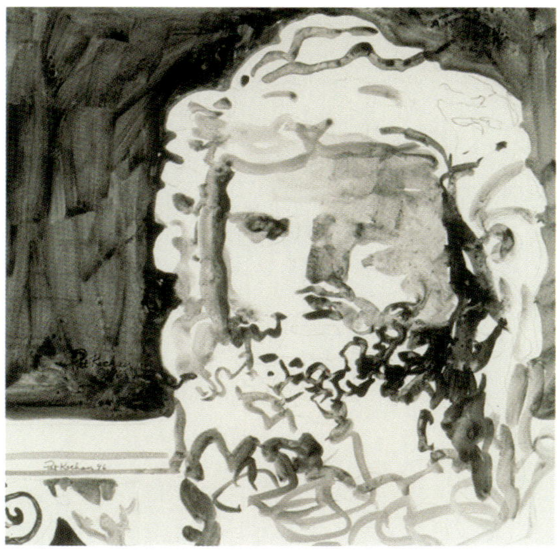

Adolphus Close-up

watercolor
13x13

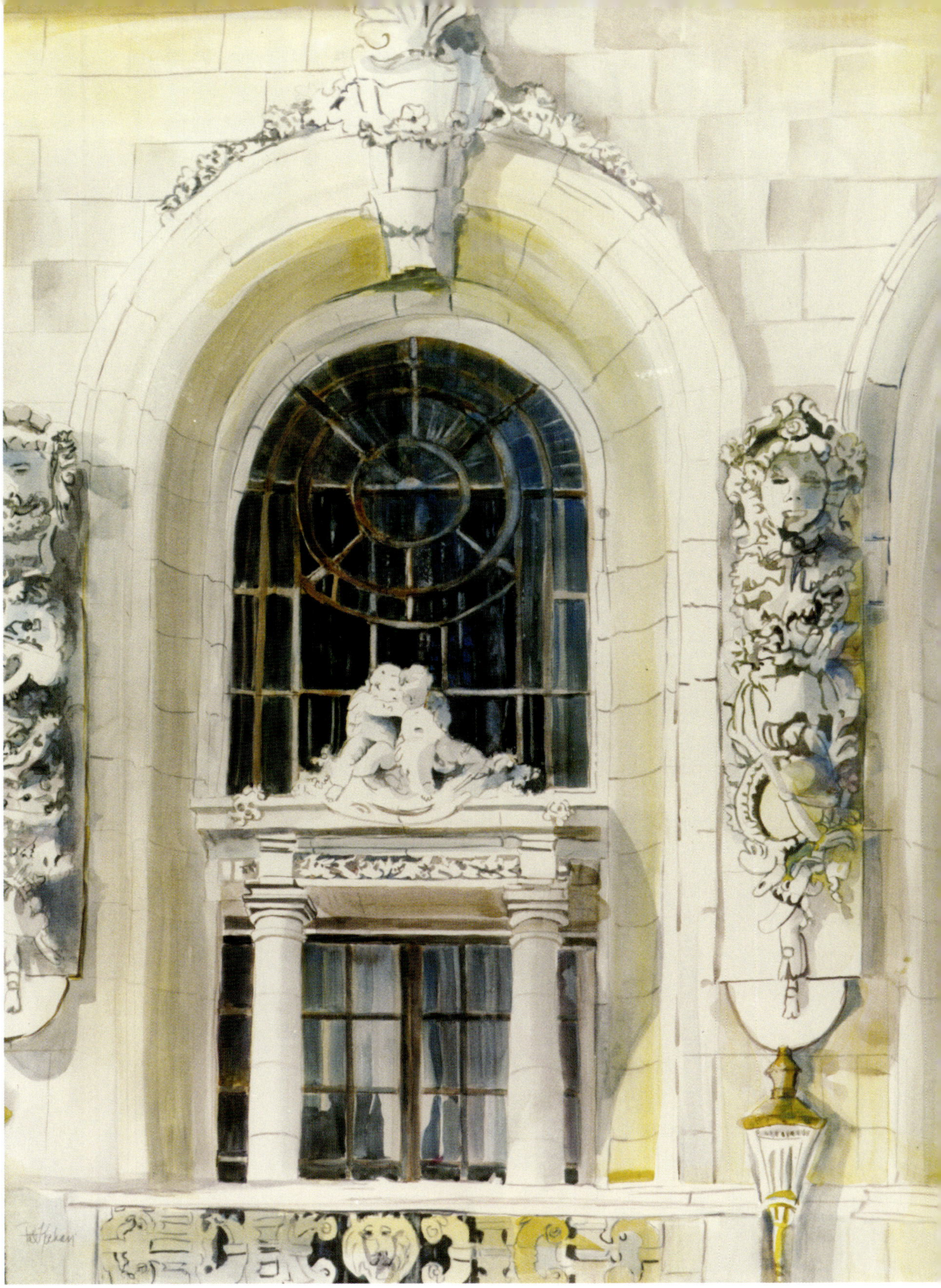

Window of Adolphus #1

watercolor
40x30

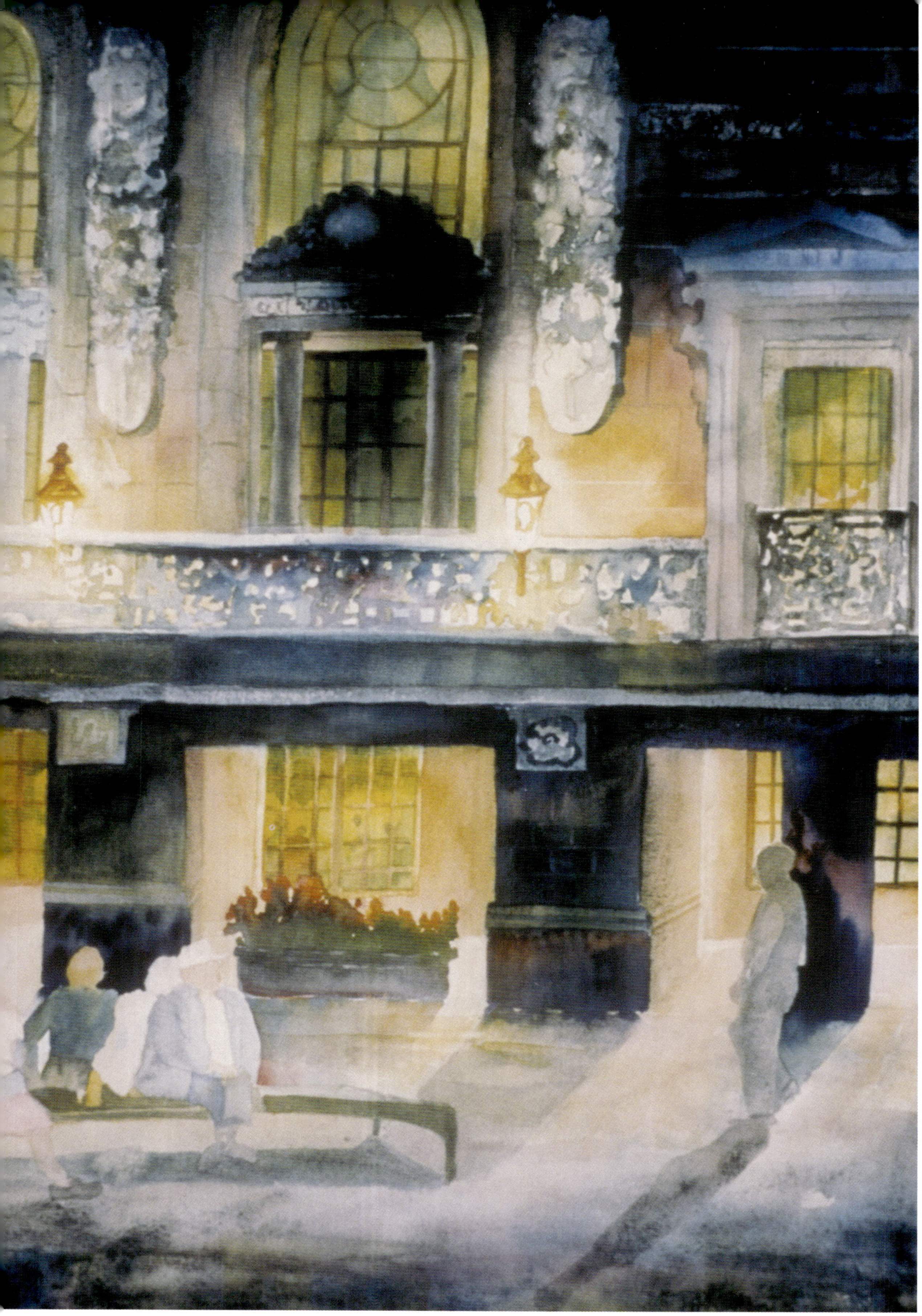

Adolphus at Night

watercolor
30x22

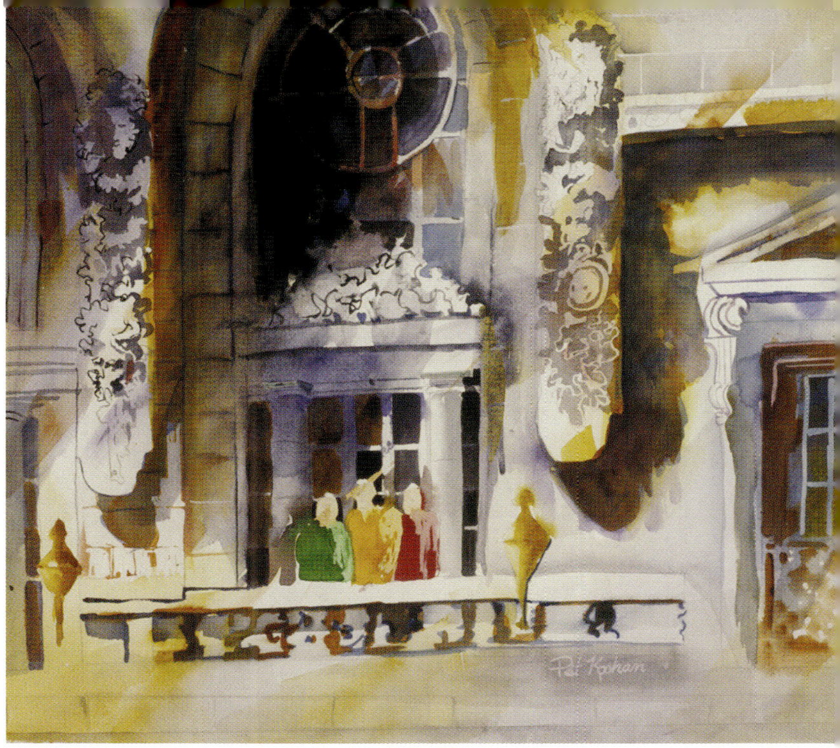

Watching the Parade from the Adolphus

watercolor
22x22

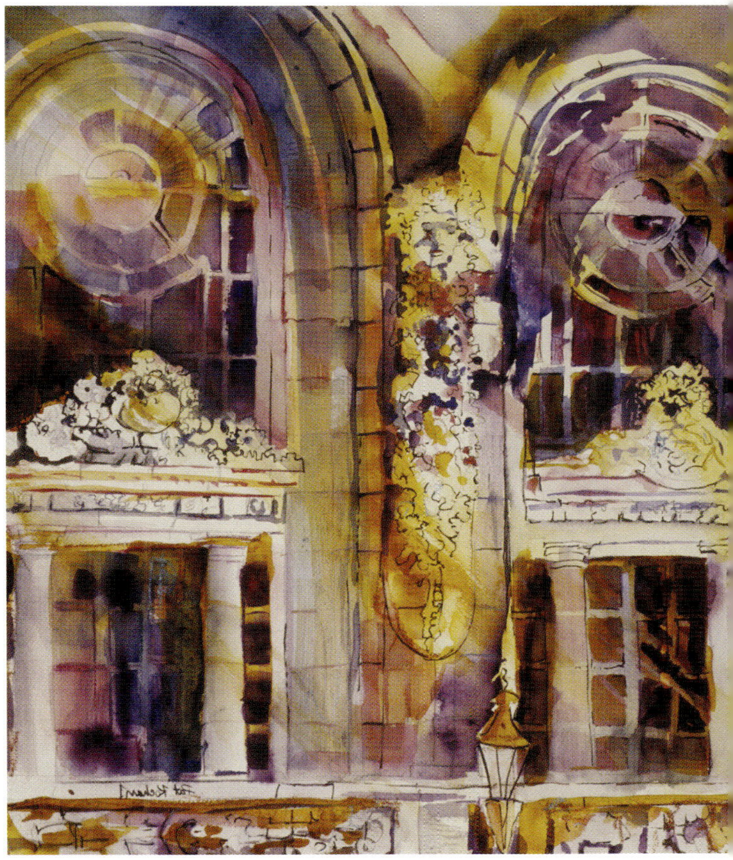

Adolphus Windows

watercolor
15x22

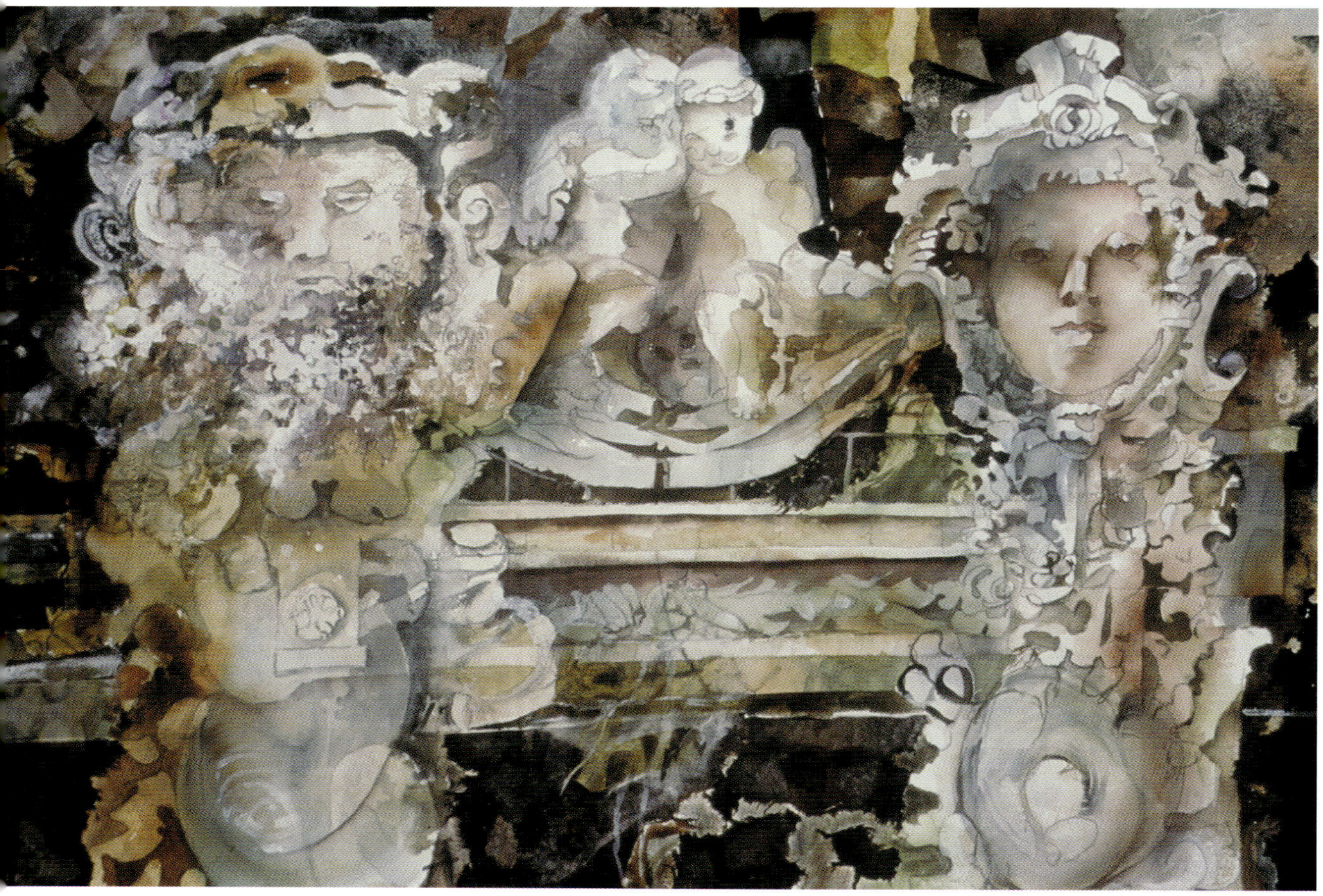

Adolphus Collage

watercolor collage
22x30

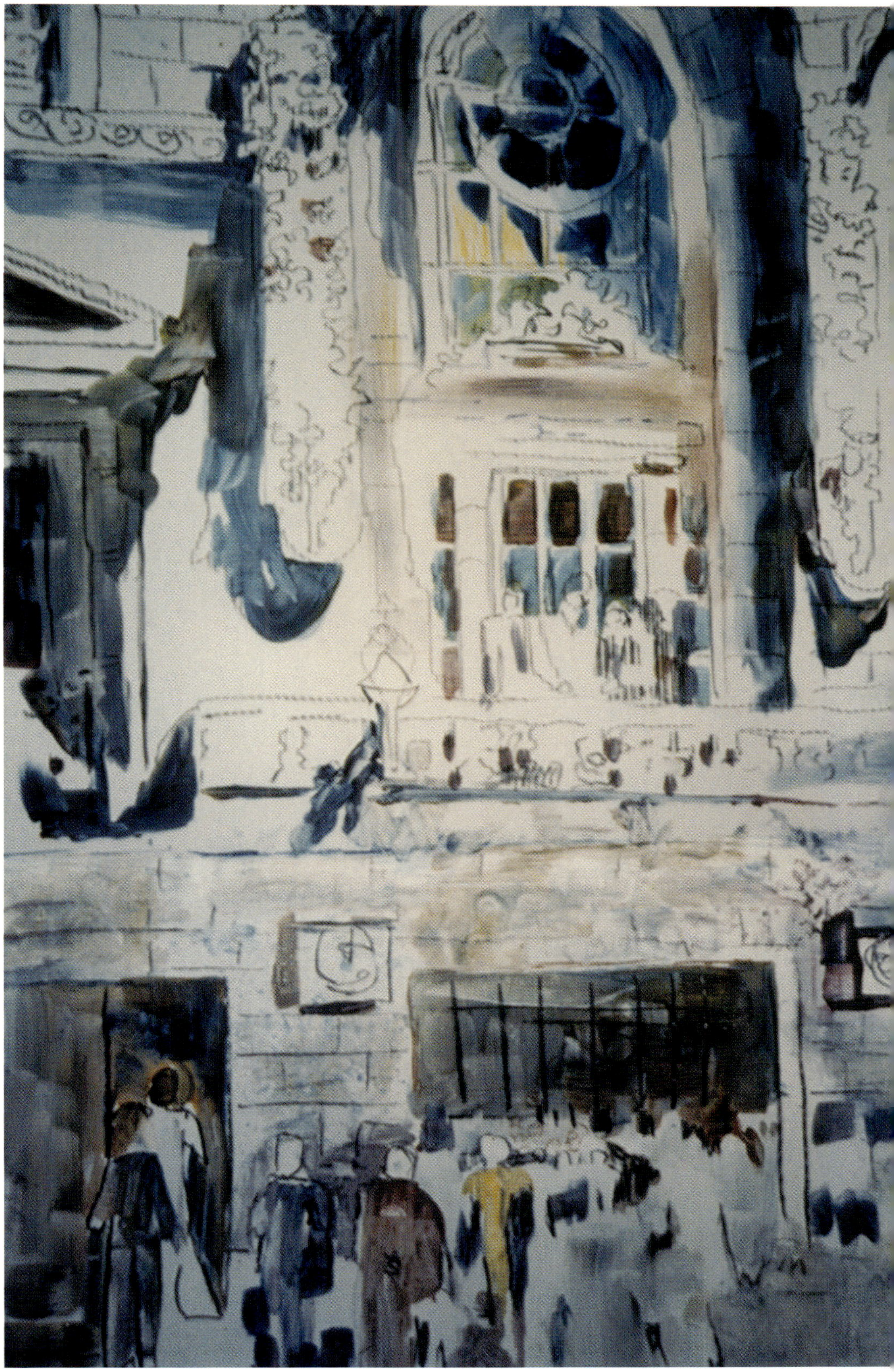

Adolphus Monotype

artist print
30x22

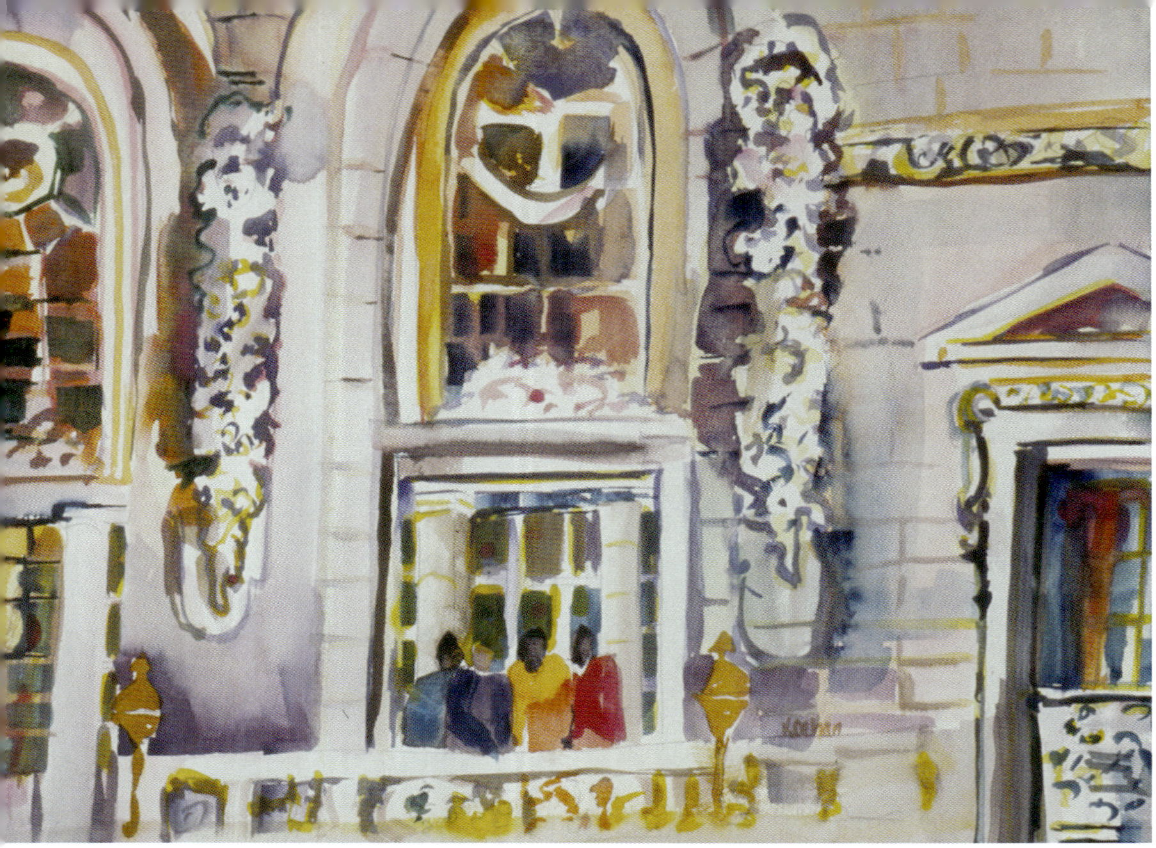

Adolphus #1

watercolor
15x22

Adolphus #16

watercolor
30x22

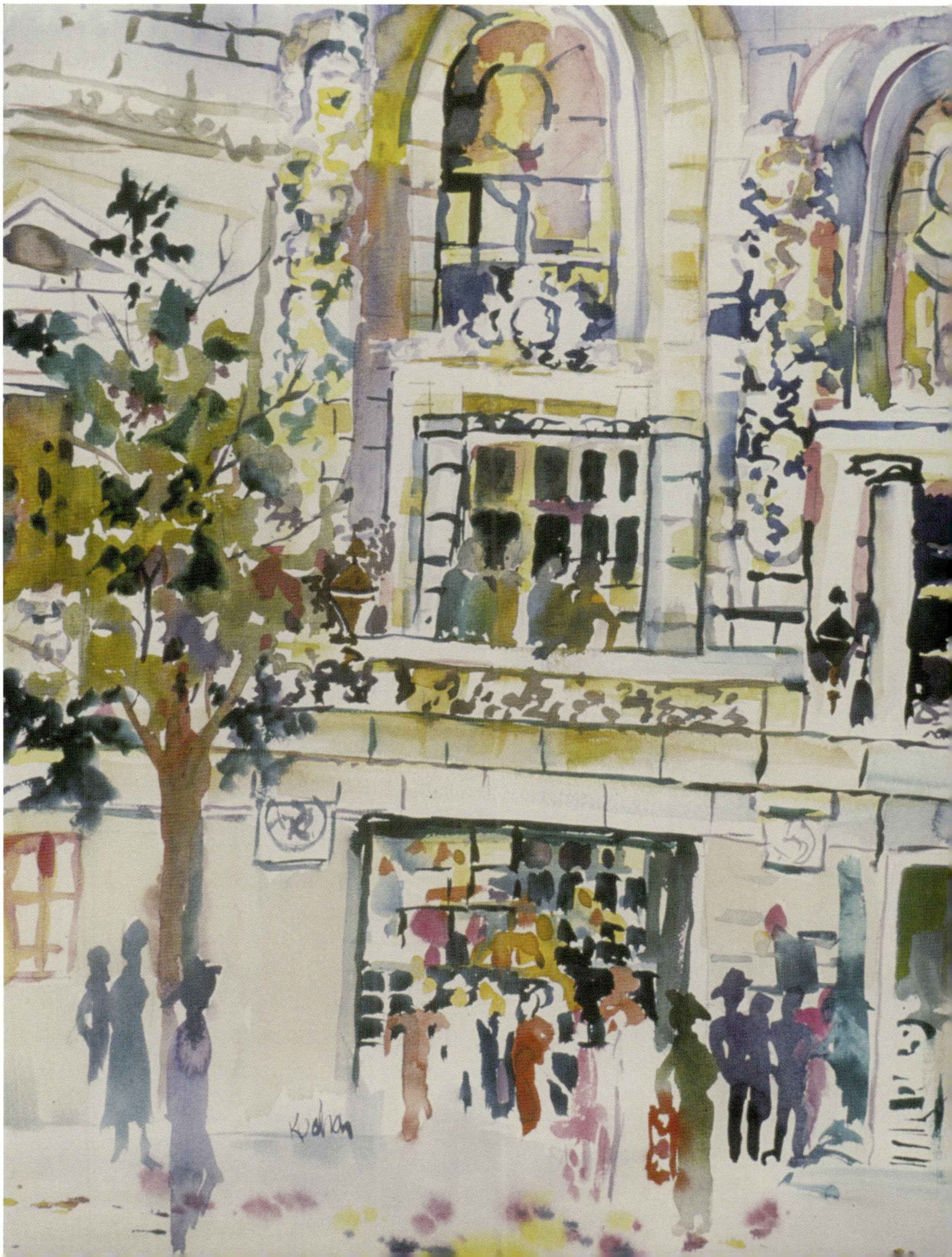

Yogurt Break

watercolor
22x30

While doing sketches for this series of paintings, I became quite amused by the scene around the Adolphus Hotel. There was a little yogurt shop nearby, and women of all sizes and shapes from the surrounding offices would stream in and out of the shop during lunch breaks eating yogurt.

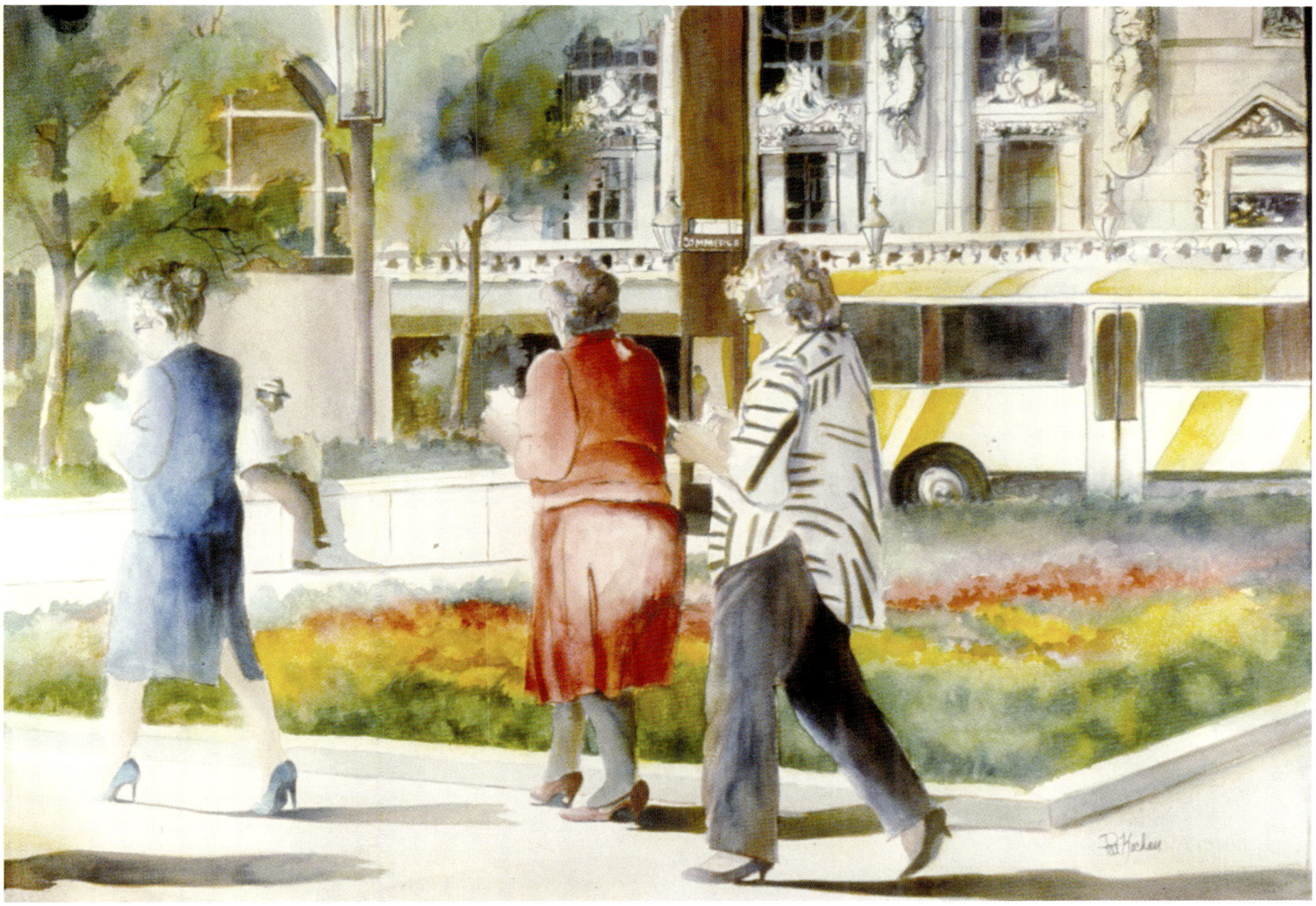

Bus Stop Red

watercolor
22x30

This painting is a prime example of artistic license. The building behind the people waiting for the bus resembles the Adolphus and includes motifs from some of the other buildings.

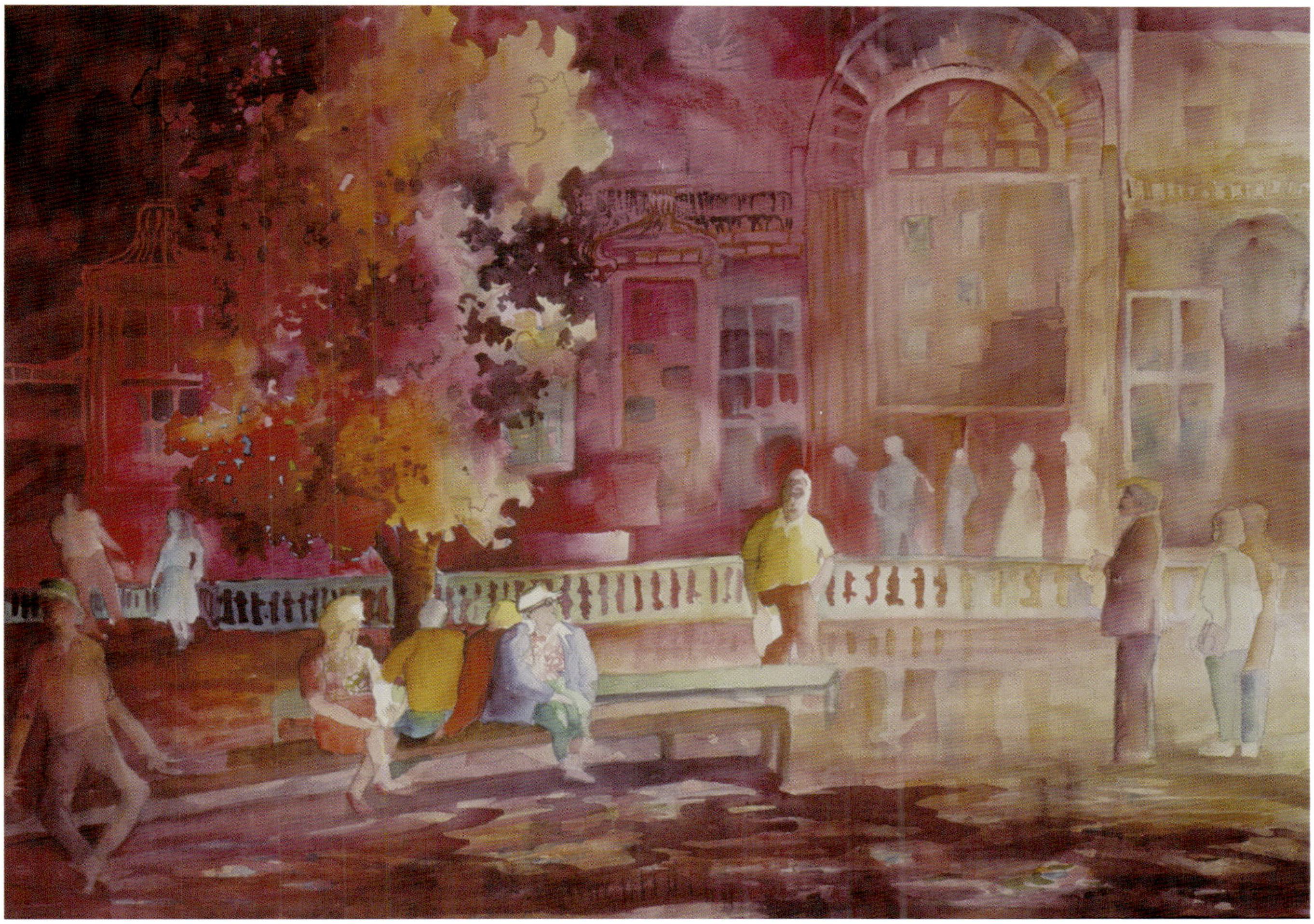

Elm Street Shopping

I remember these department stores:

Baker Shoes
Volks
La Modes
Lerner Shops
Titches-Goettinger
E. M. Kahn Co.
A. Harris
Sanger Brothers (later merged with A. Harris and became Sanger-Harris)

When I was growing up, my mom and I would dress up, ride the streetcar downtown, shop both sides of Elm Street, and then go to a movie. When I say "dress up," I mean hat and gloves, too. Folks never went to town without dressing up. It was just unheard of. As a teenager on a limited budget and needing many shoes of different colors for all of my activities, I would shop at Baker Shoes. By the end of an evening, my feet would hurt so much. One never wanted to wear those shoes for long periods of time.

A. Harris and Sanger Brothers became one. Later, Joske's purchased Titches-Goettinger. In my senior year of high school, my mom worked at E. M. Kahn, so she could afford to buy me many fine clothes for college. She was disturbed to find out that at the University of Colorado we wore cut-off Levi's most of the time. My new wool skirts and matching cashmere sweaters were seldom worn.

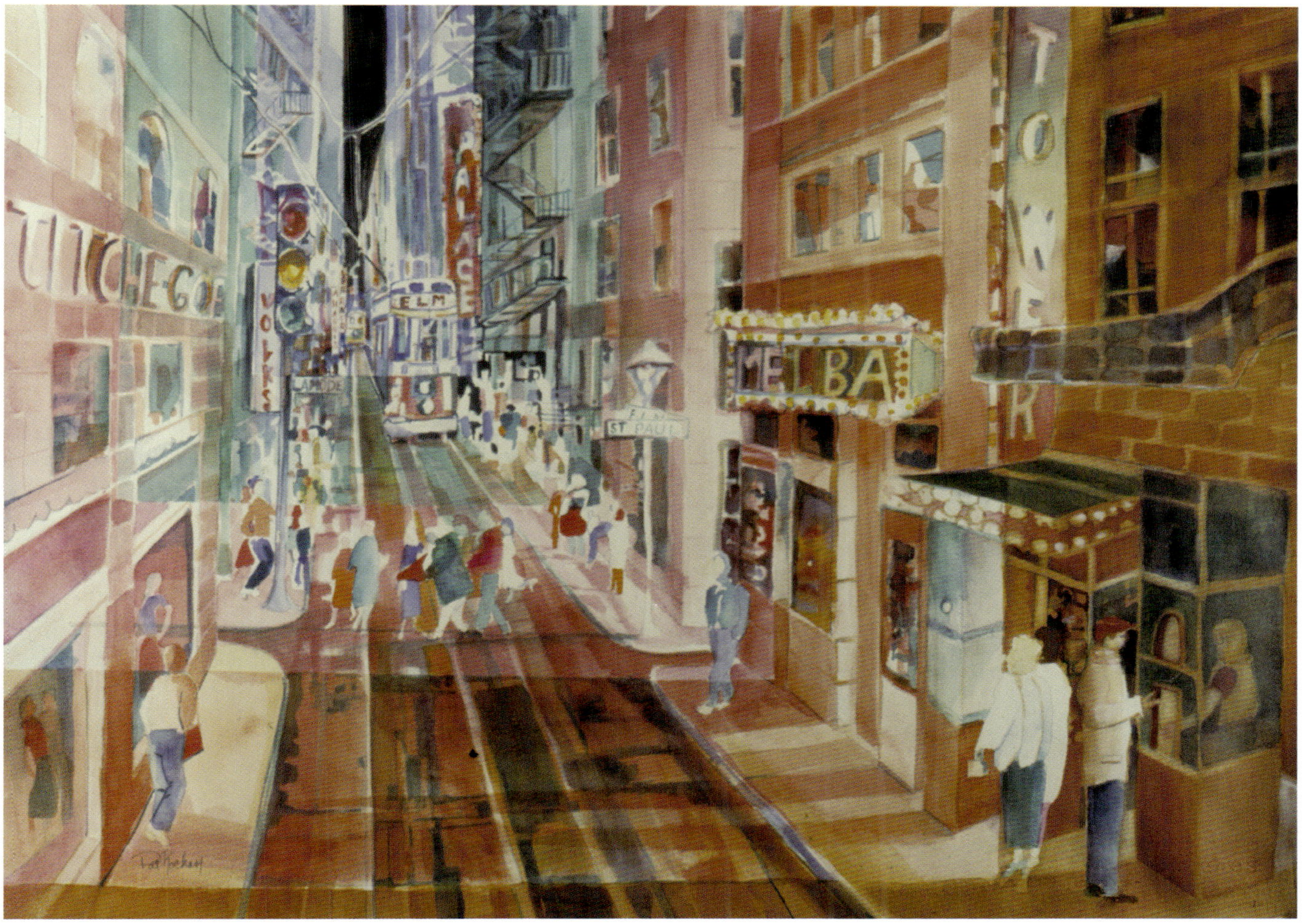

Elm Street in the '50s #3

watercolor
22x30

The Elm Street in the '50s series of paintings was composed strictly from memory. Some people referred to the street as "Theater Row" because of the movie theaters that lined the east side of the street. I have been told that I have the Melba and Tower Theaters in the wrong place, but this is my memory. The Tower Petroleum Building, to which my dad moved his office, was nestled between the Melba and Tower Theaters. The Majestic Theatre was at the end of Theatre Row. The Palace Theater was my favorite spot because at the beginning and end of the featured movie an organ would come up from below the floor, and the organist would play great music.

Note that Titches-Goettinger Department Store is on the left and other shops, such as Volks, LaModes, and others are not visible in this painting.

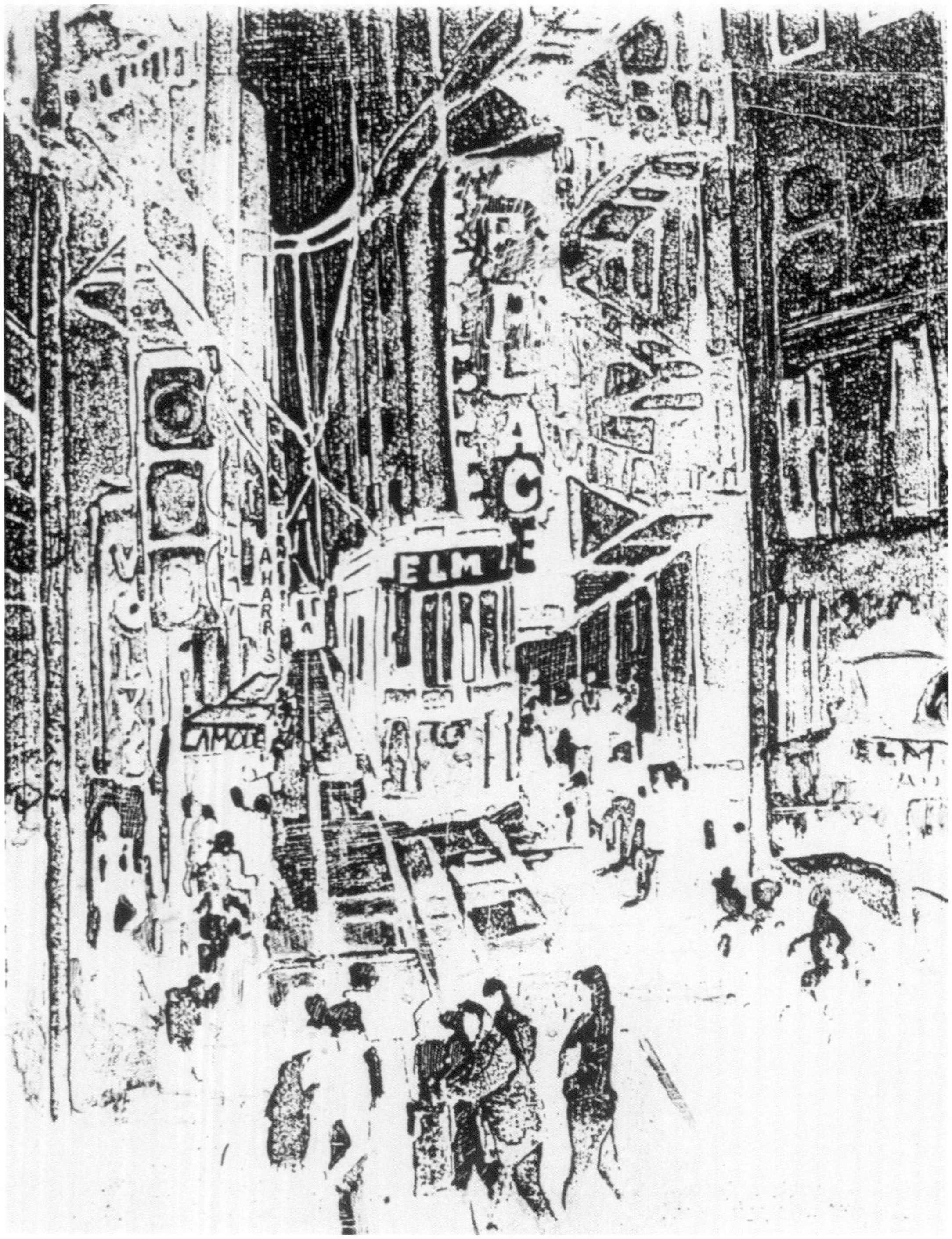

Elm Street in the '50s

artist's solar print
15x11

This small solar print is a close-up of a section from within the other Elm Street in the '50s paintings.

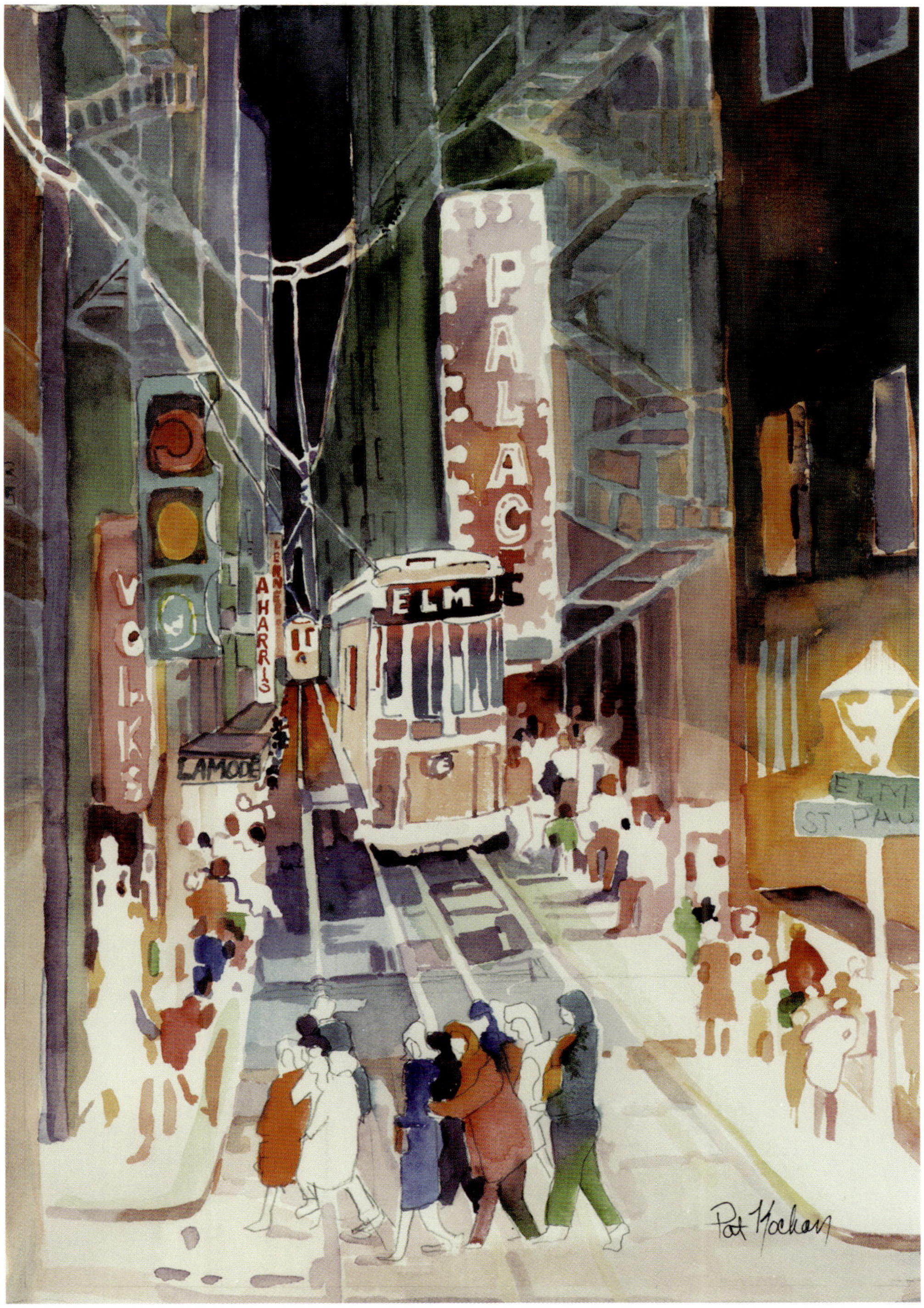

Elm Street Close-up

watercolor
15x11

After painting several pieces from my memory of Theater Row, I focused on the streetcar and people rather than the buildings. In the 1950s, there were always many people downtown, having dinner or going to the movies. We almost always ran into people that we knew because everyone went downtown for entertainment.

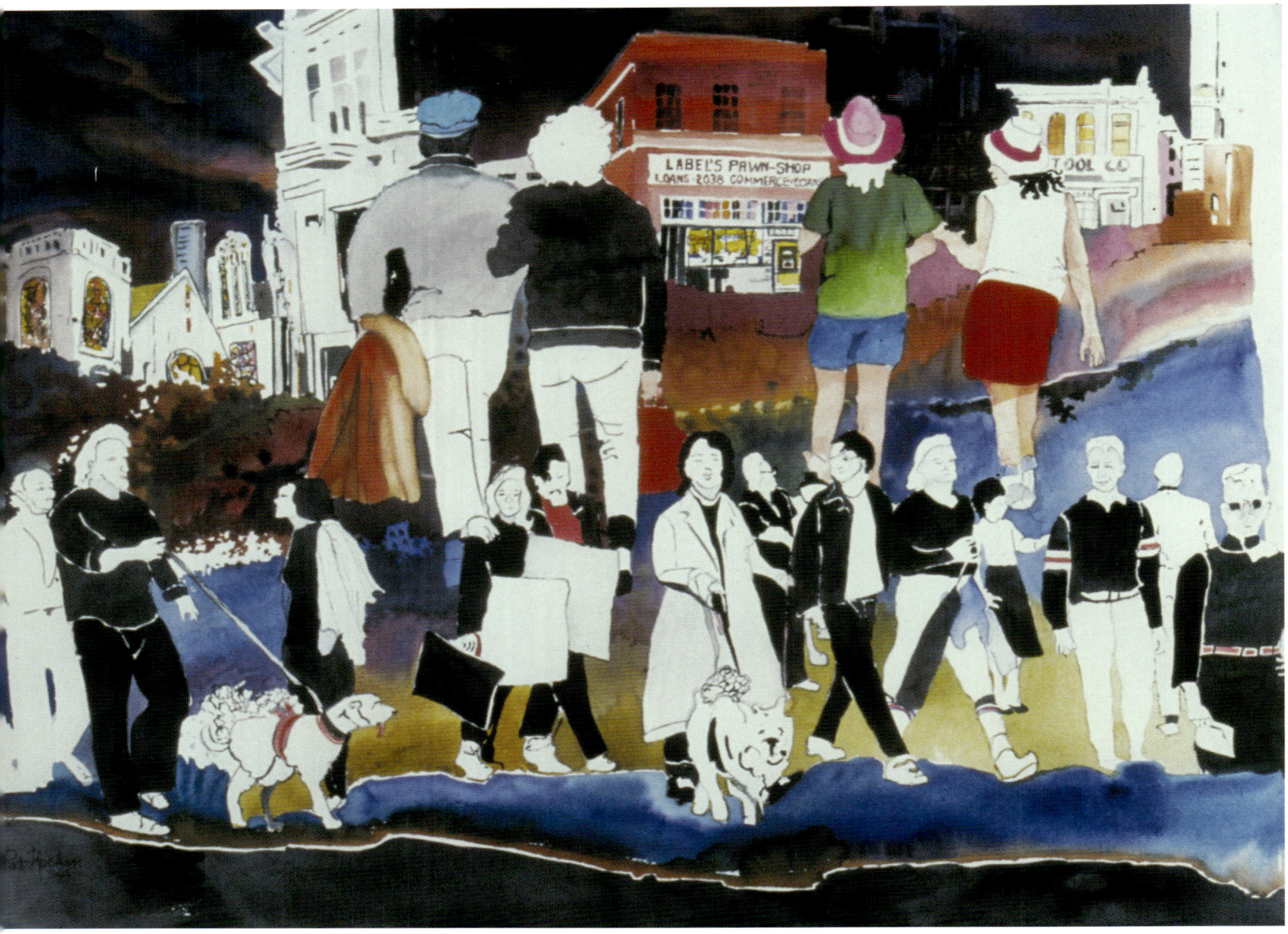

Business as Usual

watercolor
22x30

This painting evolved from my sketchbook and portrays the many gestures of people in the down-town setting. Several of these people were in a parade down Akard Street. In the background on the left is the First United Methodist Church on Ross Avenue, and in contrast on the right is an empty building on Elm Street.

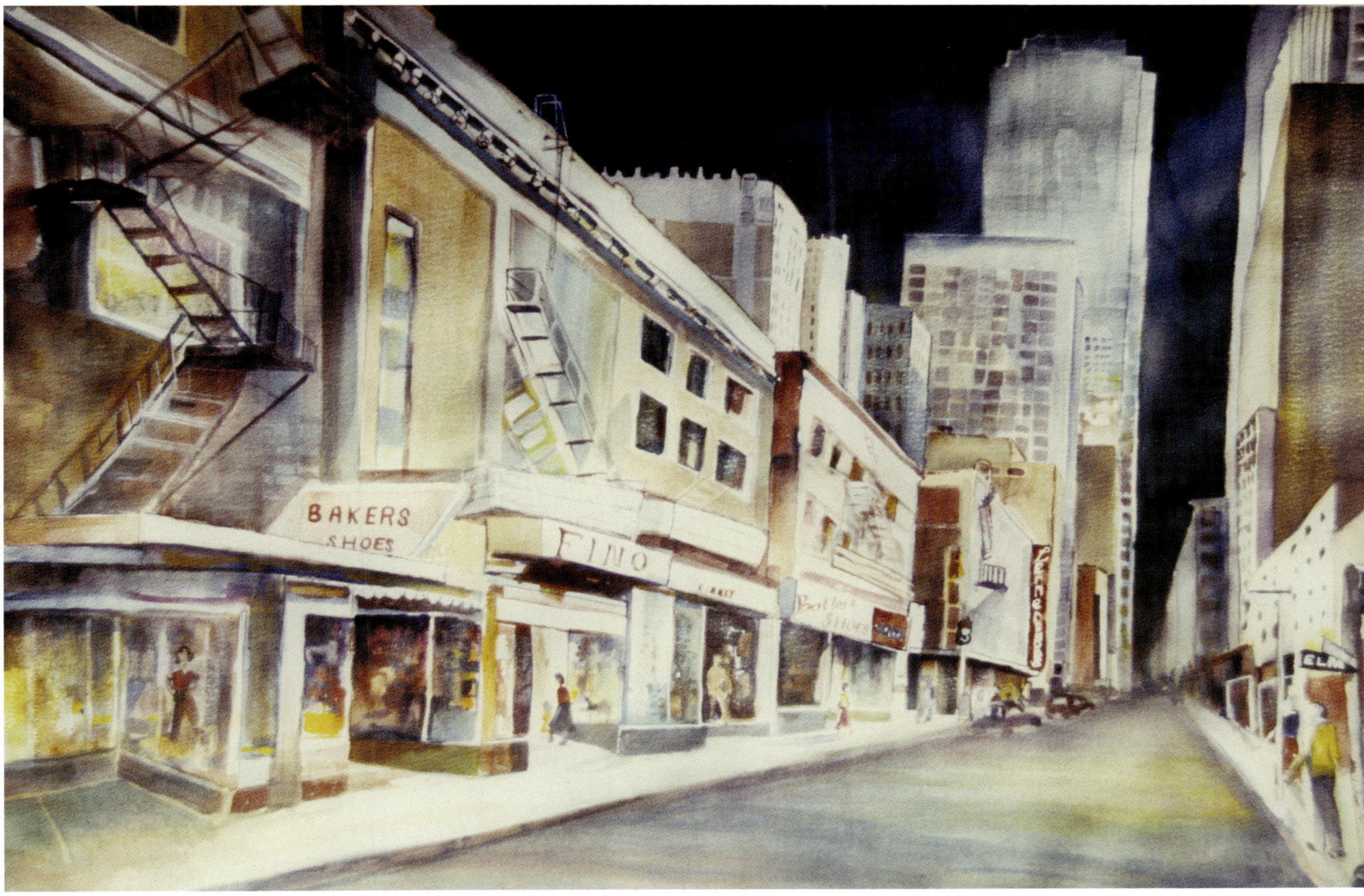

Elm Street #1

watercolor
22x30

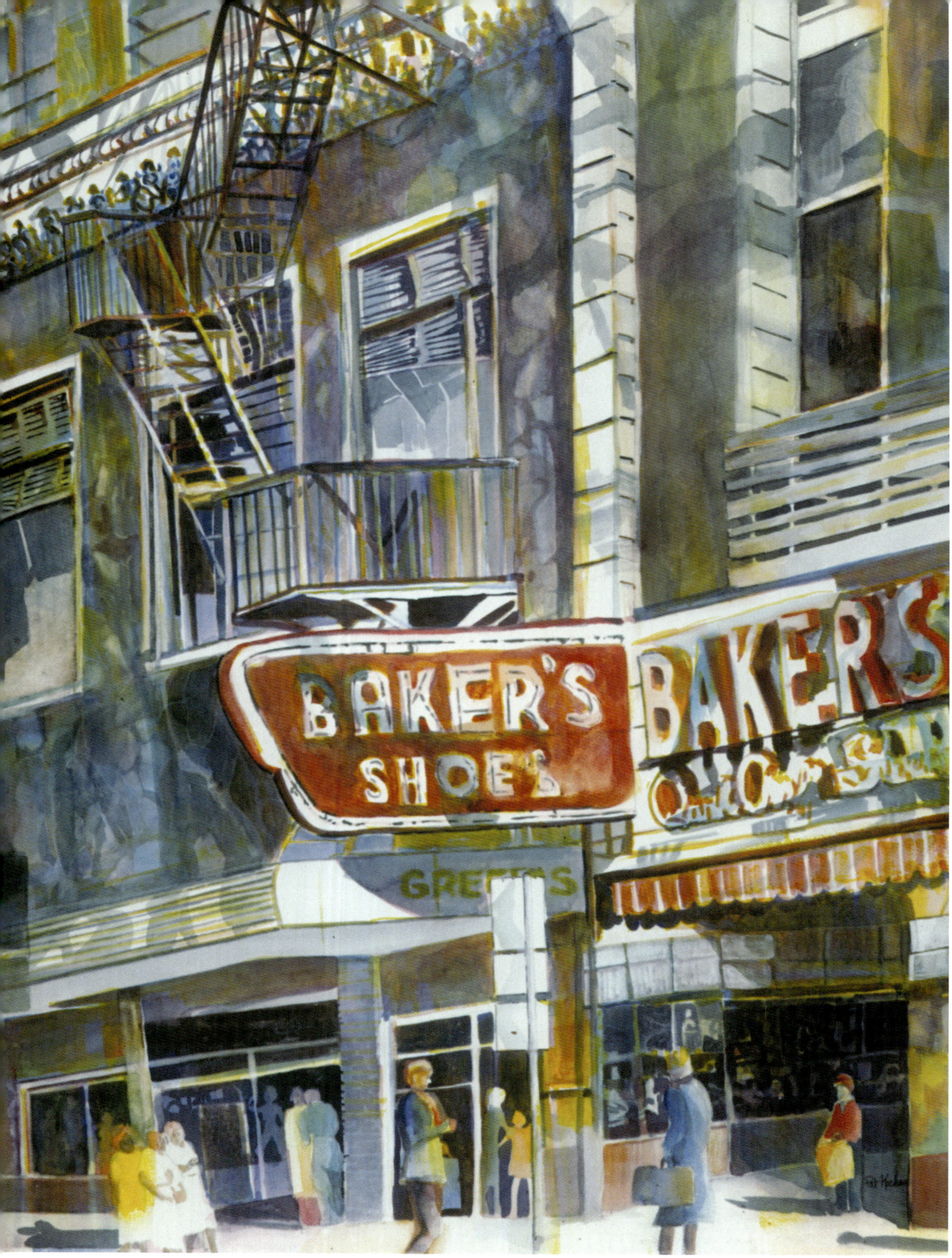

Baker's Shoes/Elm Street

watercolor
48x38

Lerner Shops/Elm Street

watercolor
32x42

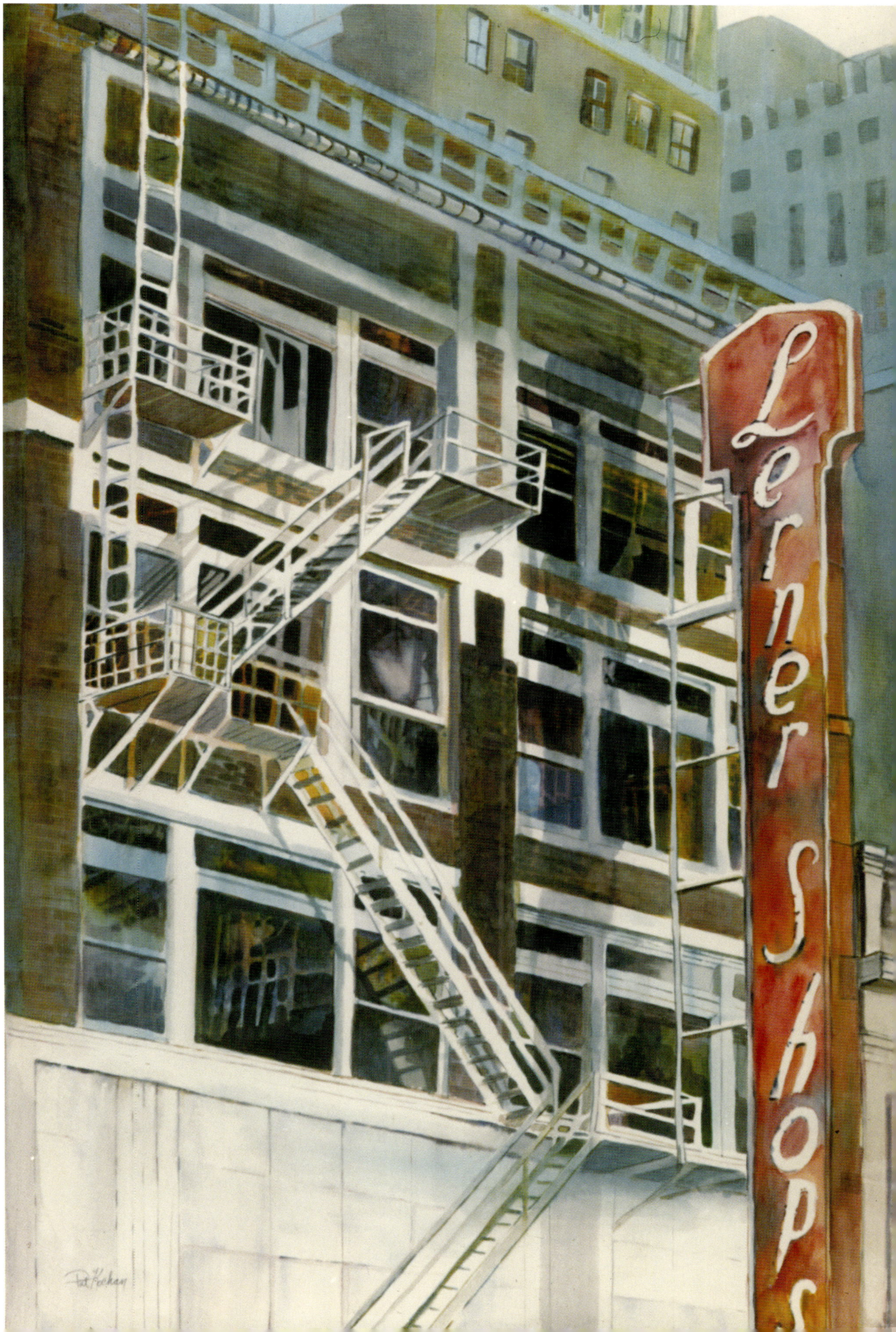

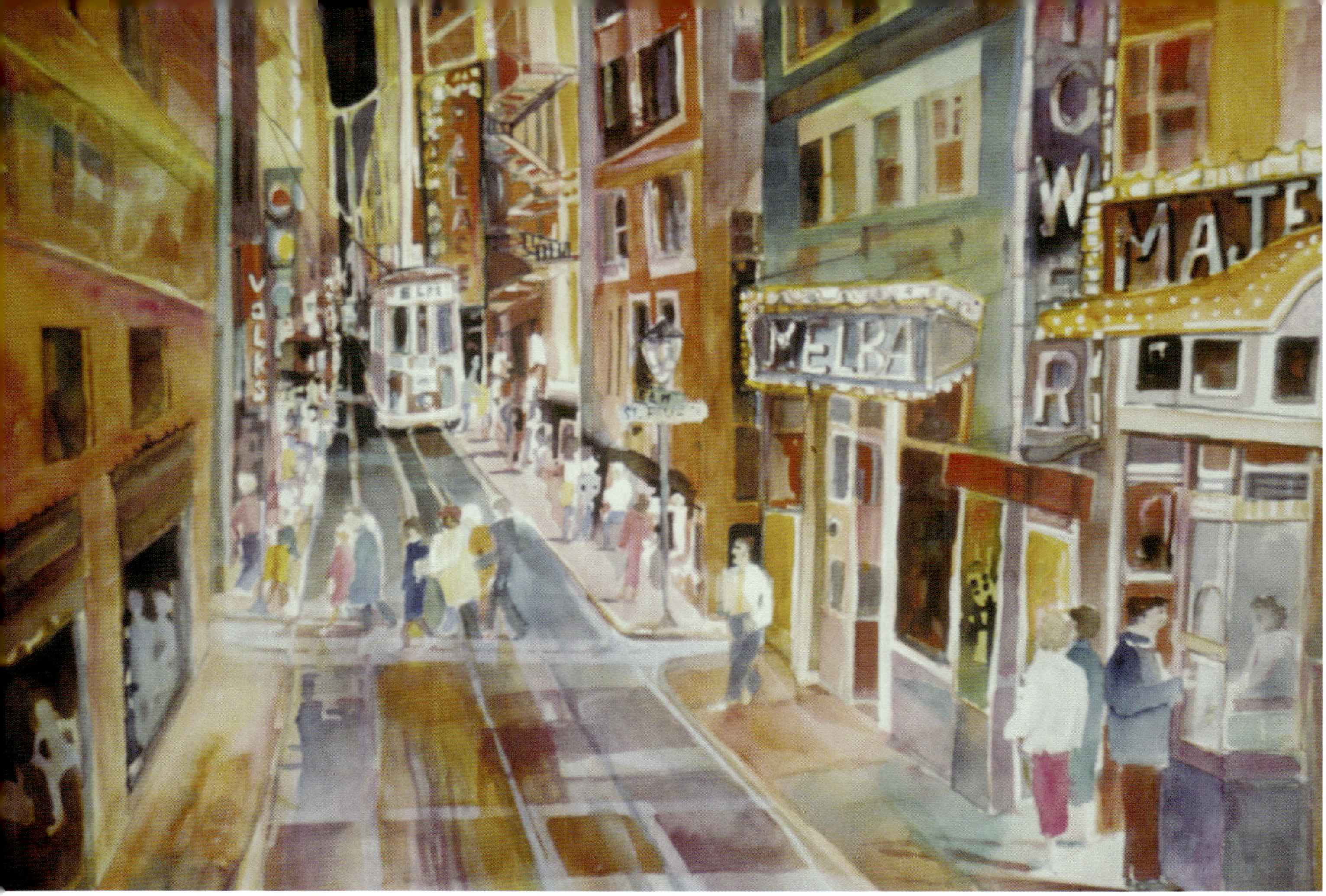

Elm Street #2

watercolor
22x30

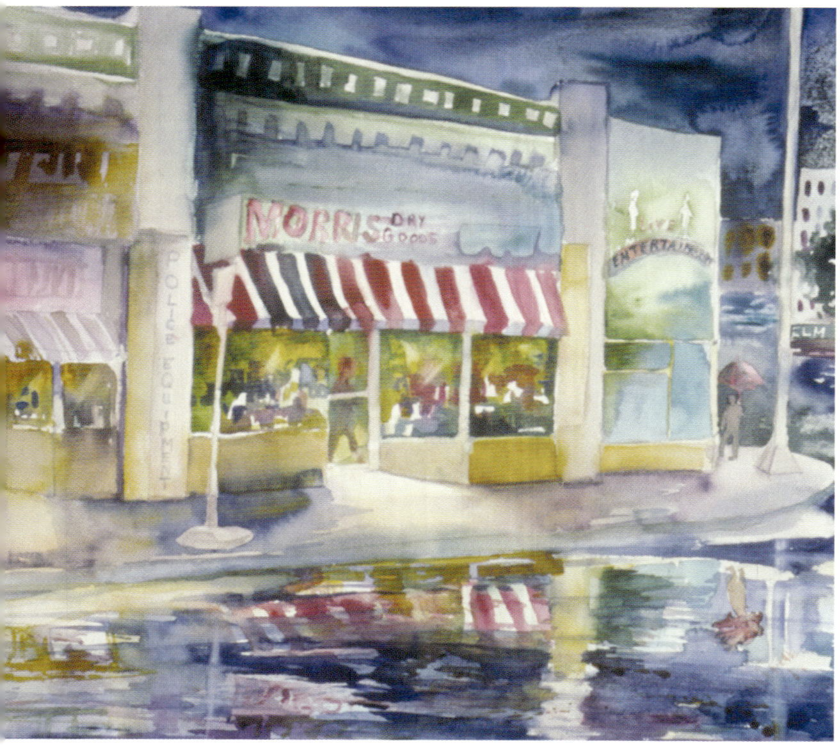

Last Standing Shopping Strip

watercolor
25x25

I painted this shopping strip on Elm Street several times. This time, in 1998, I painted it at night with a wet street and lighted windows. The wet street mirrors the illumination of the windows in the darkness. The painting on the opposite page is another view of the same shopping center. The business on the end changed owners frequently.

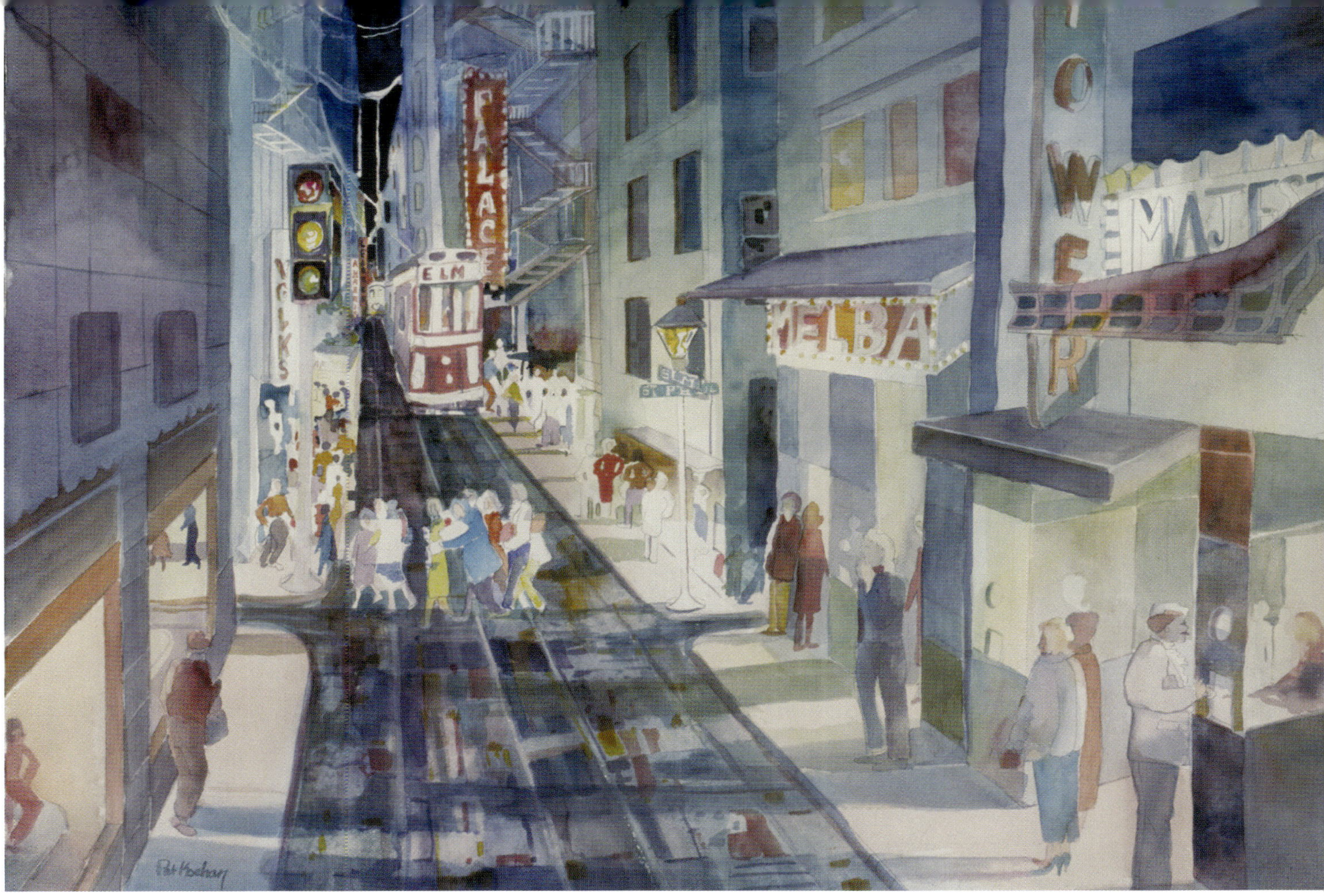

Elm Street in the '50s #4

watercolor
22x30

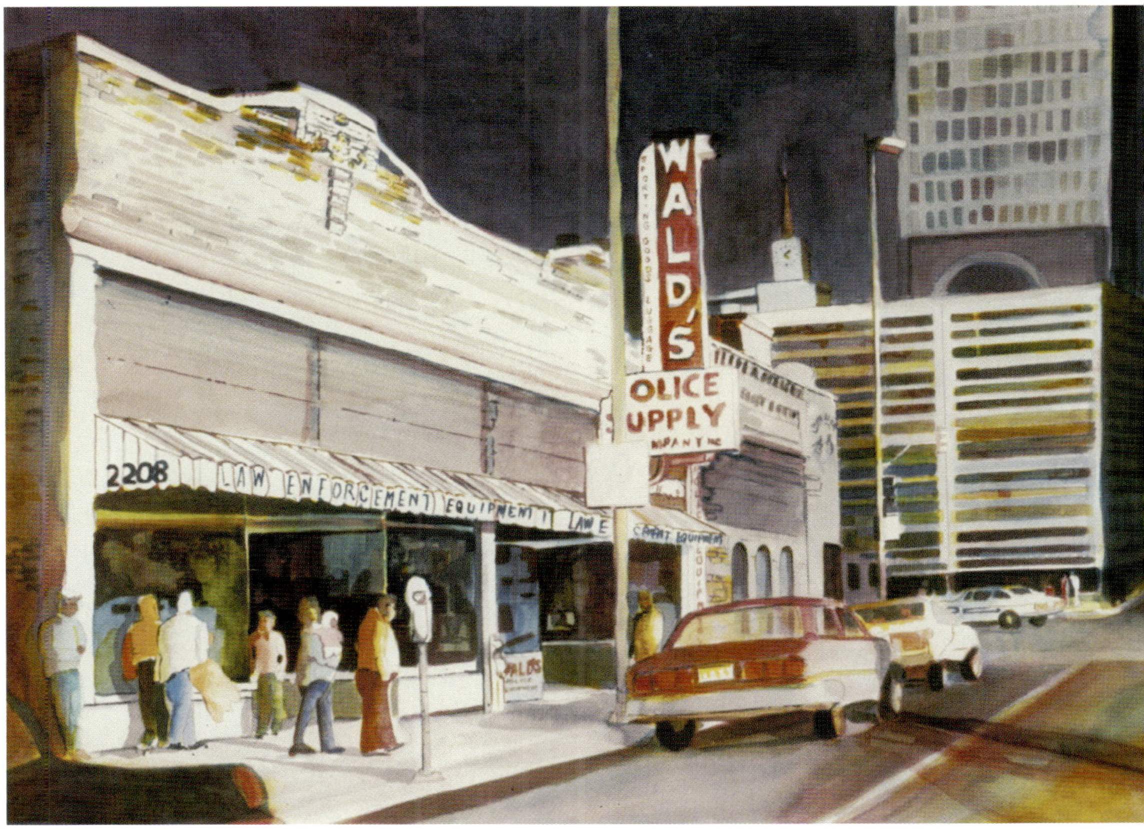

Wald's on Elm Street

watercolor
22x30

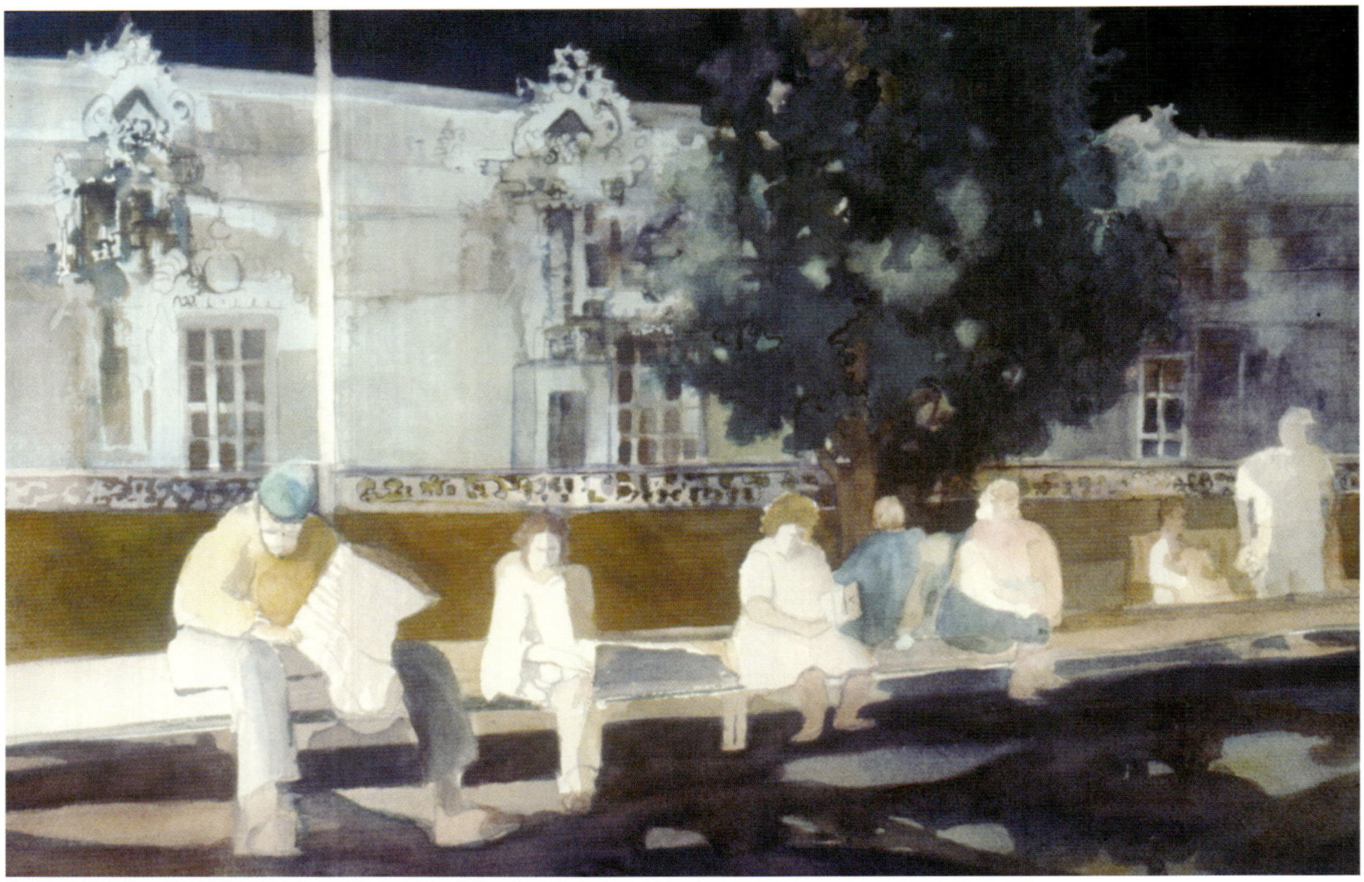

Bus Stop 1

watercolor
22x30

At this bus stop, I observed that strangers sat in close proximity but never uttered a word to one another. Each person was totally engrossed in his or her own thoughts. The moment seemed unfriendly and lonely to me. The building behind the figures is from my imagination but is greatly inspired, once again, by my love of the Old World sculptures from the Adolphus and Magnolia buildings.

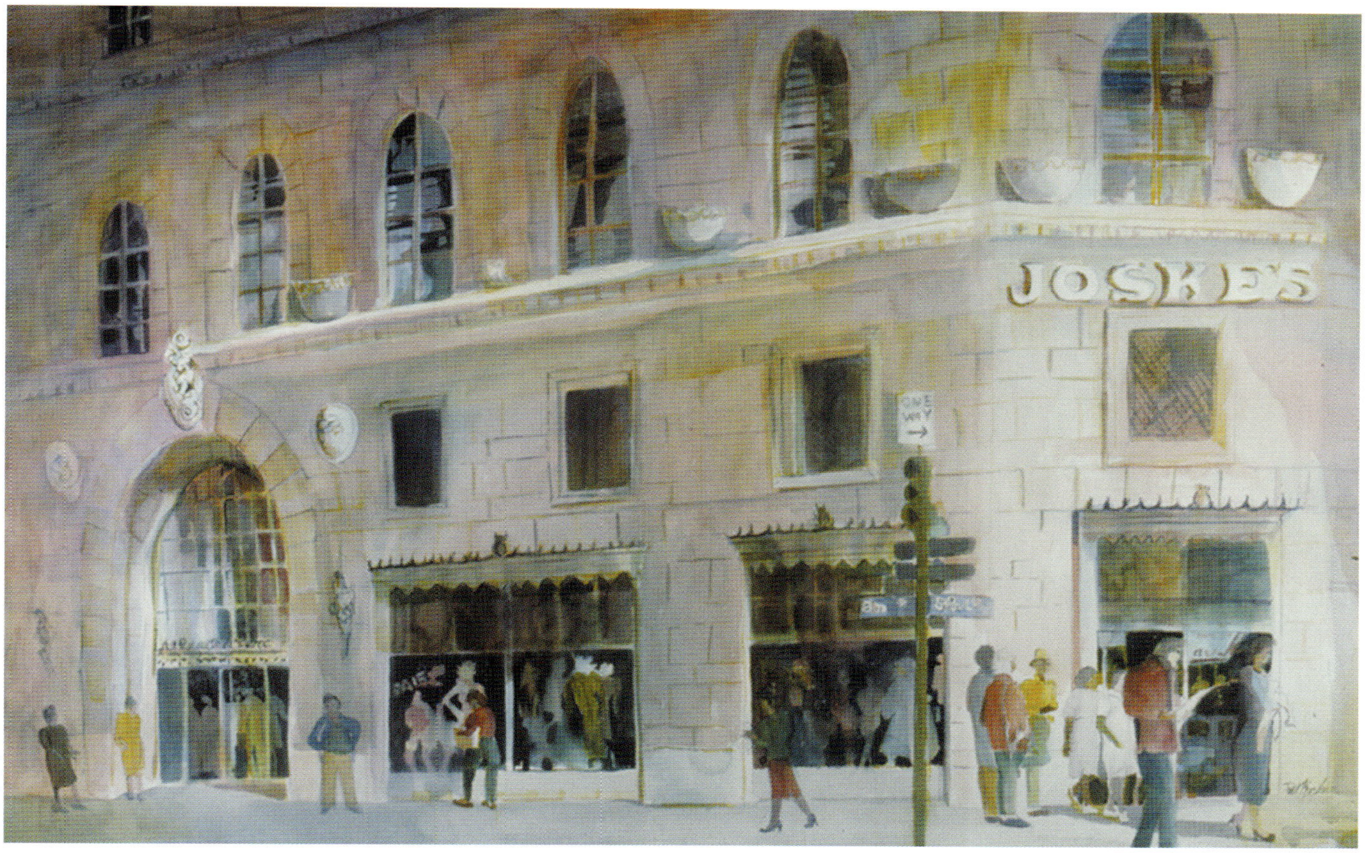

Joske's

watercolor
32x48

This store was named Joske's Department Store at the time this was painted. Growing up, I knew it as Titches-Goettinger Department Store. My mom shopped for "piece goods," as they were called then, which meant fabric and material for sewing. It was an interesting store, and my mom especially liked going to the bargain basement.

Downtown People Diptych

watercolor/ink
22x30

The people in these paintings came from my sketchbook. In the upper picture, there are three maids waiting for a bus in front of Joske's, and the street person on the left with his bag of "stuff" is eating lunch, sitting by the fountain in Bell Plaza. My husband, John, is on the left in the lower one. On the right is a beggar, who is seen in many of my paintings. I have used the couple walking with their backs to us in several paintings, especially in commissioned pieces for newlyweds.

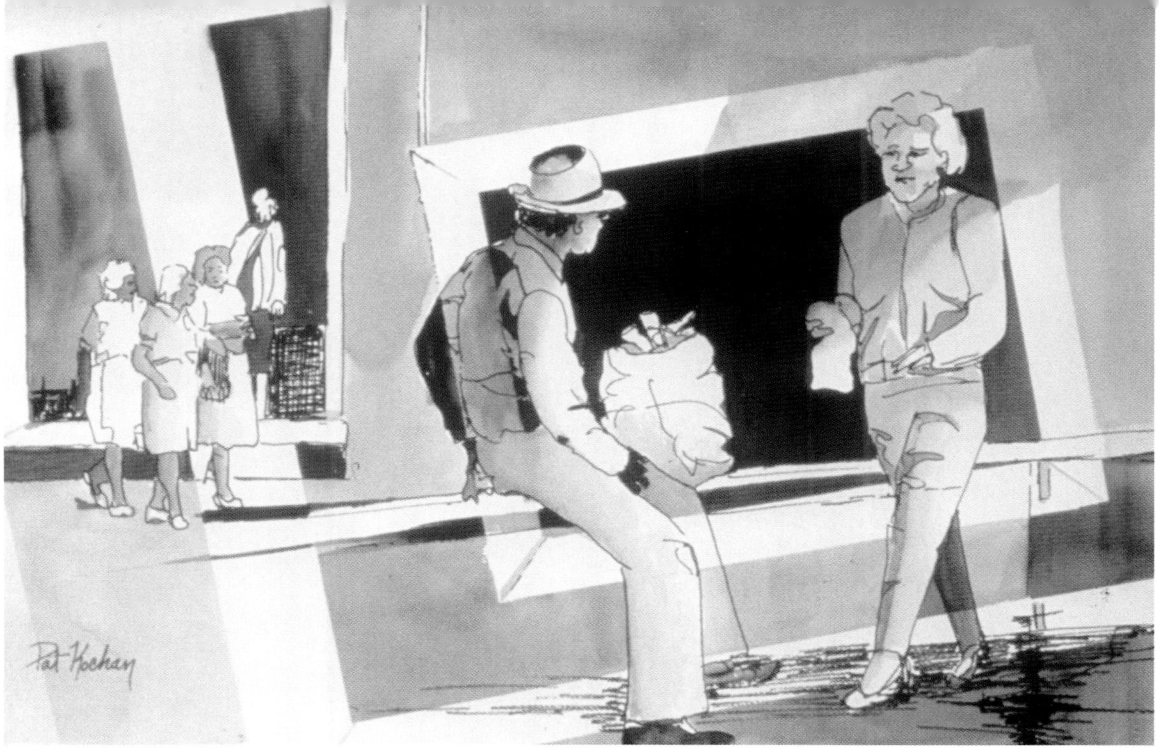
Pat Kochan

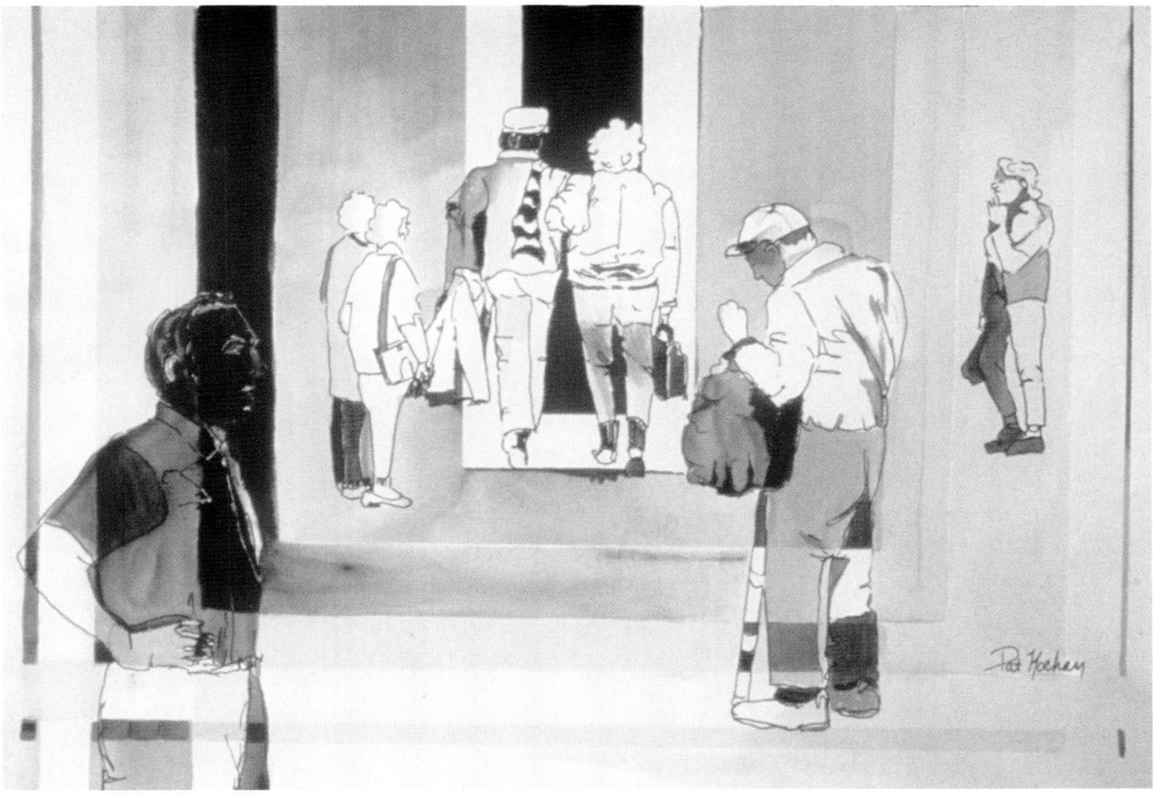
Pat Kochan

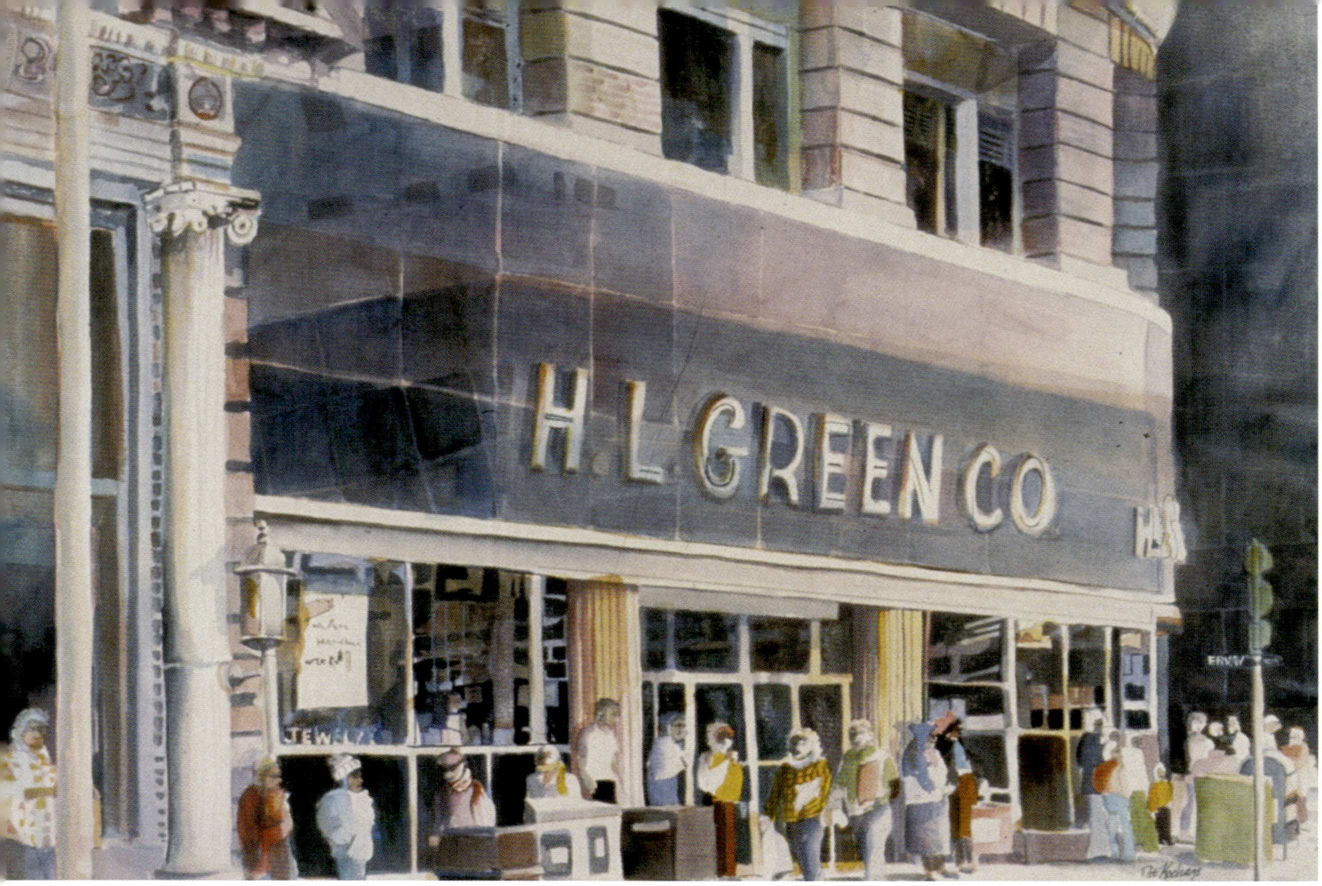

H. L. Green

watercolor
22x30

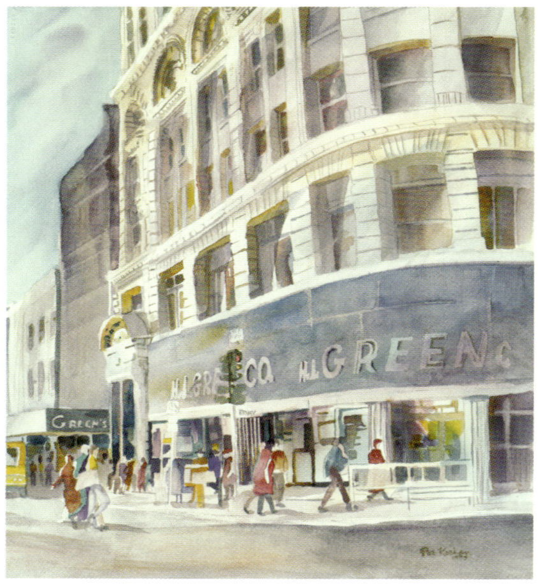

H. L. Green Remembered III

watercolor
30x22

The Wilson Building (H. L. GREEN CO.)

My childhood memory of this building is vivid. It was a dime store, as we called them then. My mom bought curtains there and other affordable items that we needed. This building still stands at Main and Ervay streets, and, thanks to the preservationists, it has been registered as a national landmark. It was built in 1903, and the architecture is modeled after the Garnier Opera House in Paris. It has been renovated for upscale housing. I have painted this unique building many times from different viewpoints.

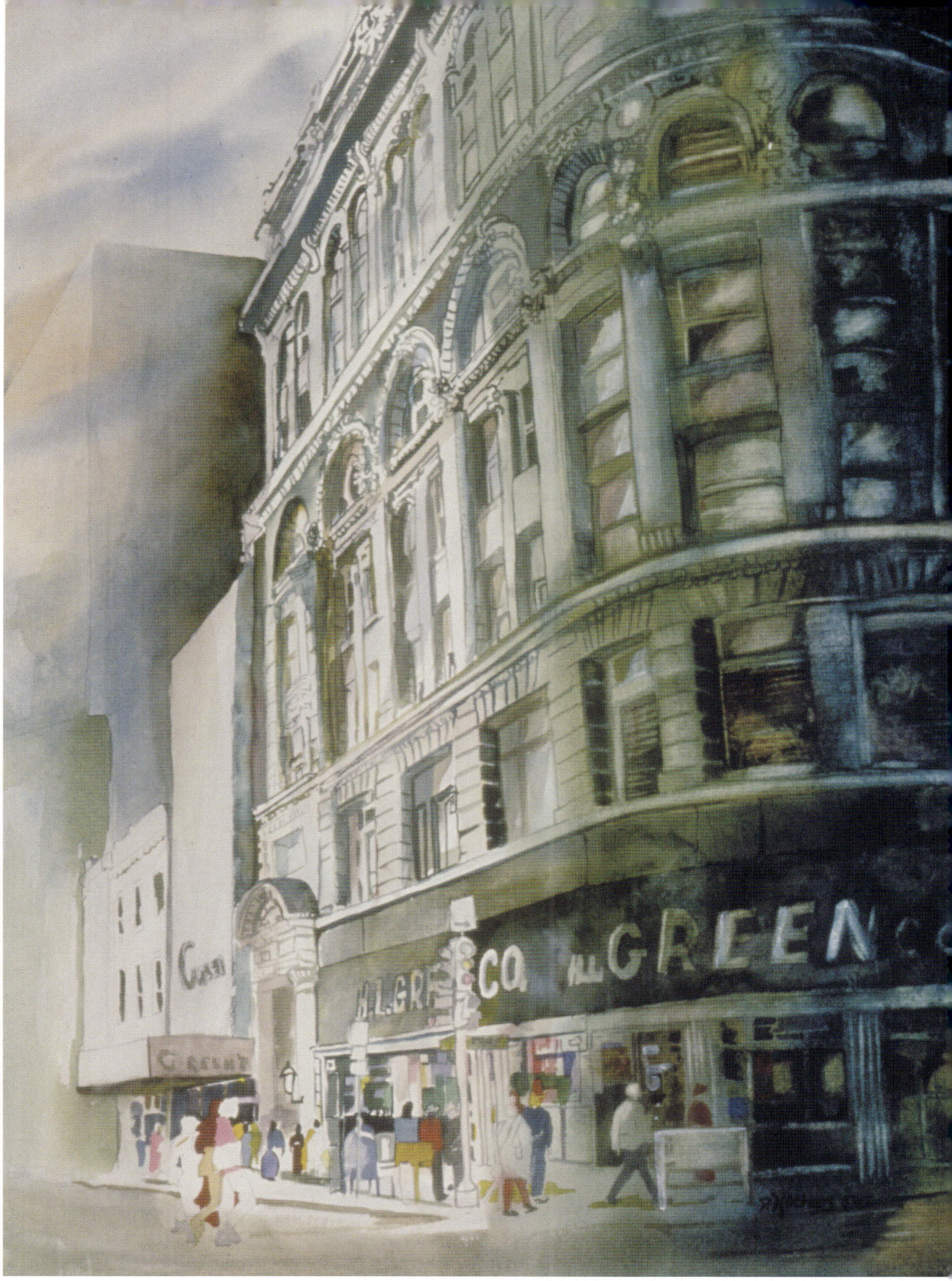

H. L. Green Retrospective

watercolor
30x22

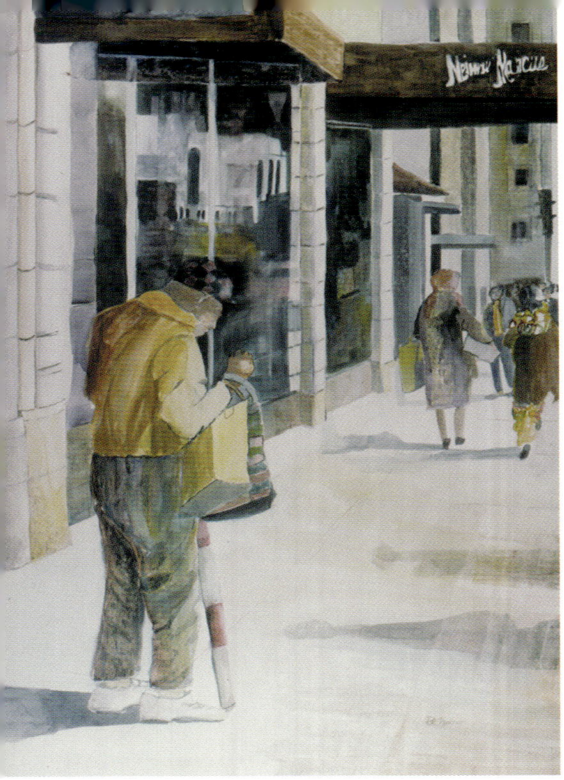

The Beggar #1

watercolor
40x30

Neiman Marcus was known as "The Best Department Store in Dallas." My mom was a wonderful seamstress. When I was a teenager, we would pick out beautiful clothing at Neiman's, try it on, and Mom would draw it and reproduce it. In those days, you could buy labels with the Neiman's name. So, all my coats and clothing had the "Neiman Marcus" label inside. Wasn't she smart? I had designer clothes without the cost.

Notice the difference between the people going in and out of Neiman's and the people waiting for a bus or going in and out of H. L. Green Co. People are wearing fur coats and high-heeled shoes at Neiman's and jeans and old coats at H. L. Green. That was when I realized as a child that some people had so much and others so little.

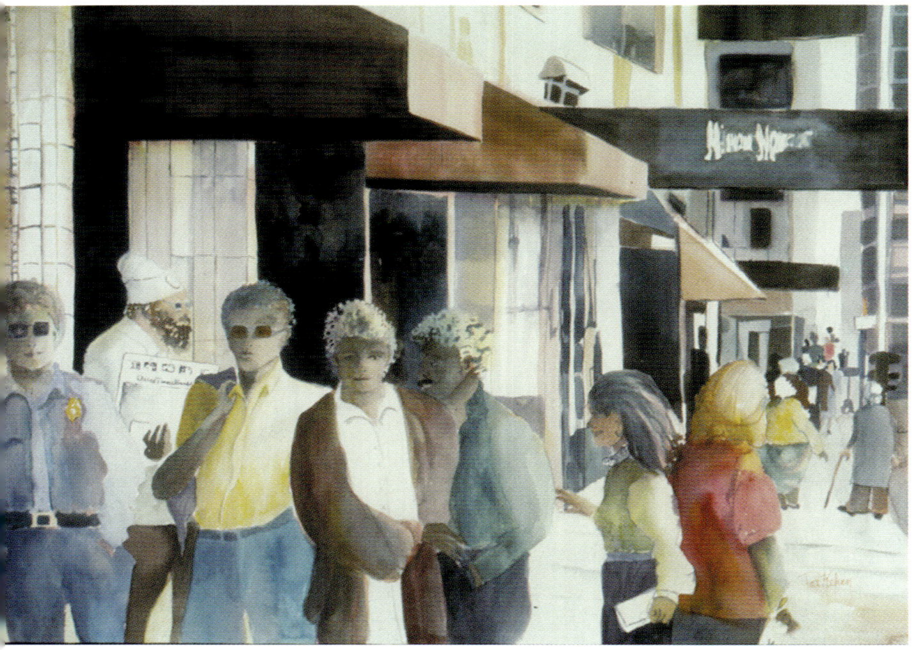

Neiman's Corner

watercolor
30x22

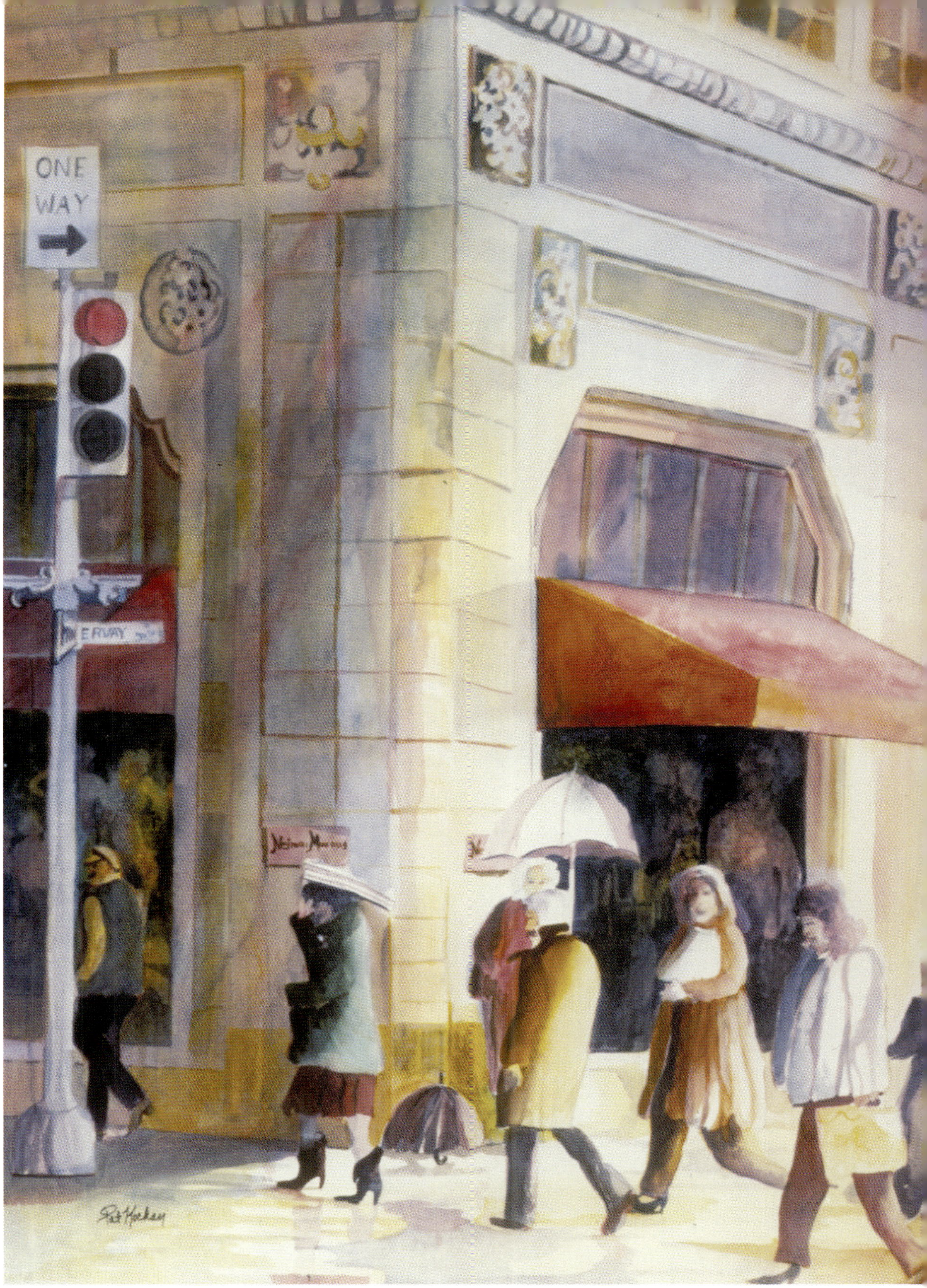

Neiman's at Christmas

watercolor
22x30

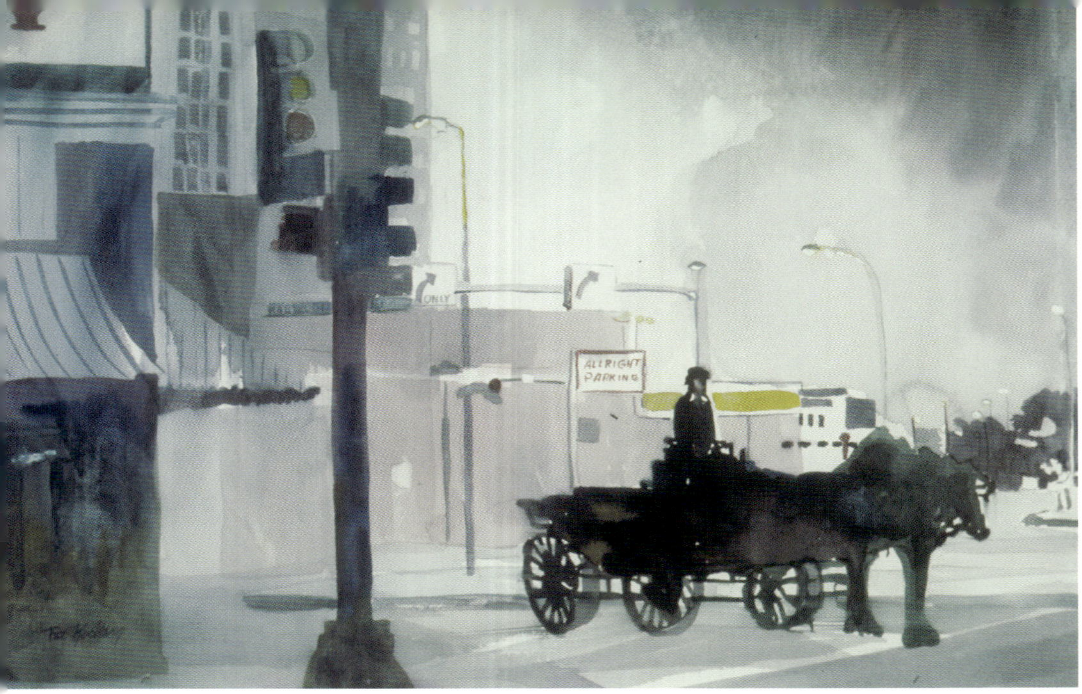

Carriage on Harwood at Elm Street

watercolor
11x15

I often saw this carriage while researching the downtown area for this series of paintings. I especially enjoyed the back lighting that particular evening just at sundown.

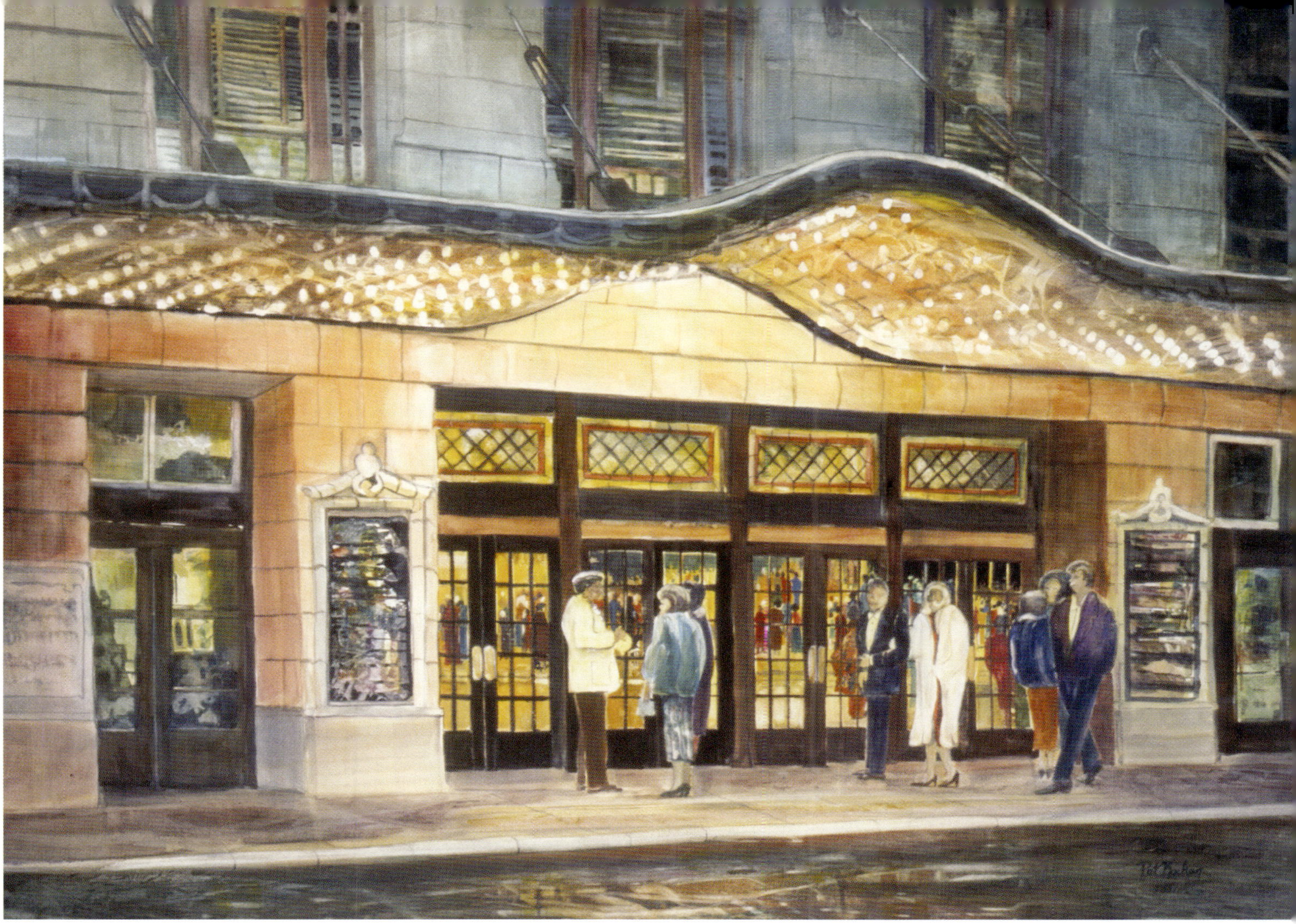

Majestic Theatre #3

watercolor
30x40

Having painted the Majestic from several viewpoints, the focus here is on people attending a play when the theater was no longer used for movies. The attire was certainly dressier for the plays than for the movies.

Majestic Theatre #2

watercolor
49x45

When I was growing up, this was a movie theater. It was not unusual to see people lined up around the block to see a first-run film. At the end of the movie, my friends and I would wait at the back stage door to have the stars of the movie sign autographs. Jimmy Durante and Vincent Price were two of my favorites because they were both such gentlemen. The Majestic is now a live theater.

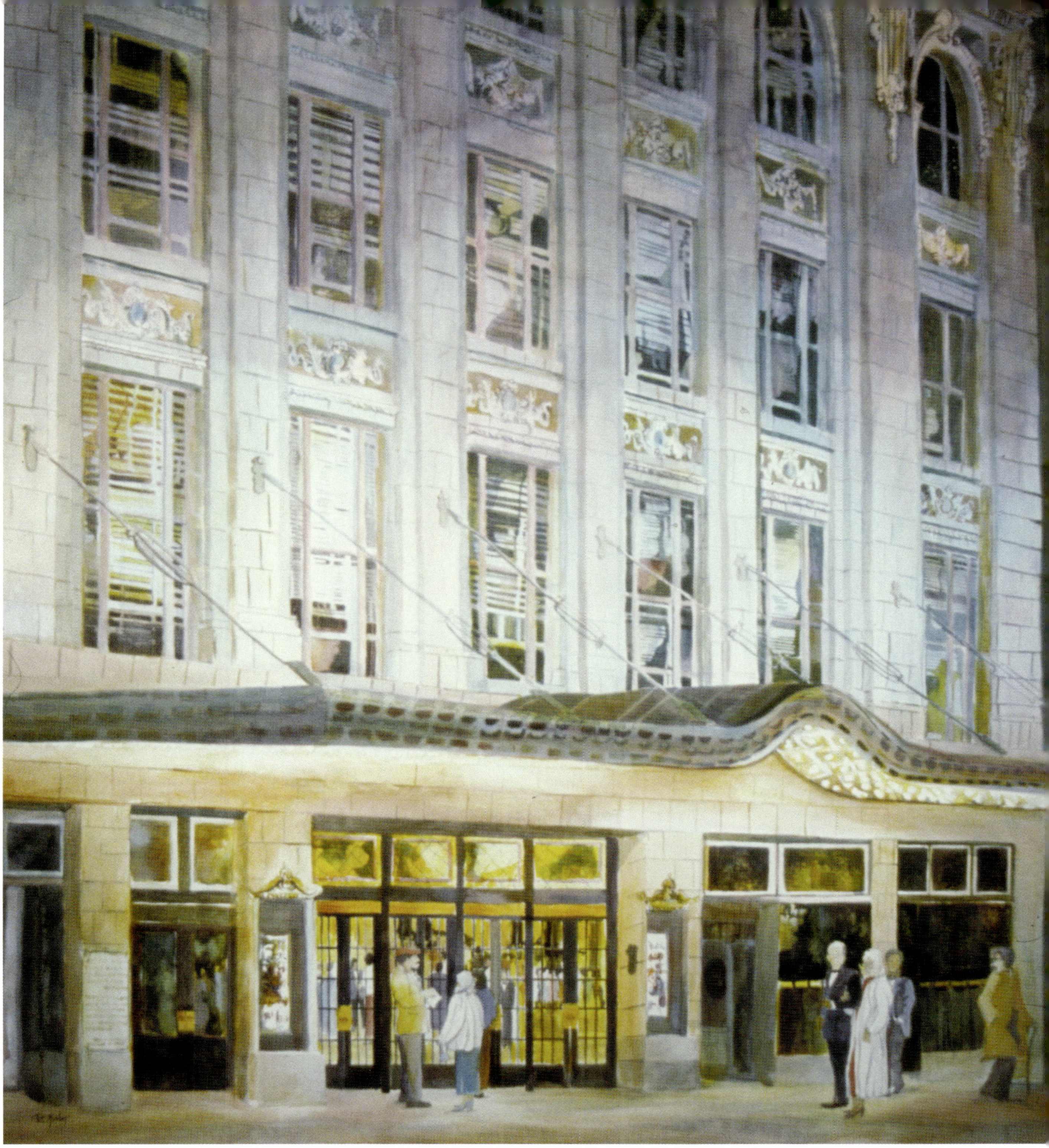

Dallas Plaza Hotel 1

watercolor
30x22

This was the first Hilton Hotel in the United States and is located at Harwood and Commerce streets. When I painted this hotel, it was named the Dallas Plaza, but it has had many other names and different colored awnings. My parents spent their wedding night at this hotel on June 19, 1936.

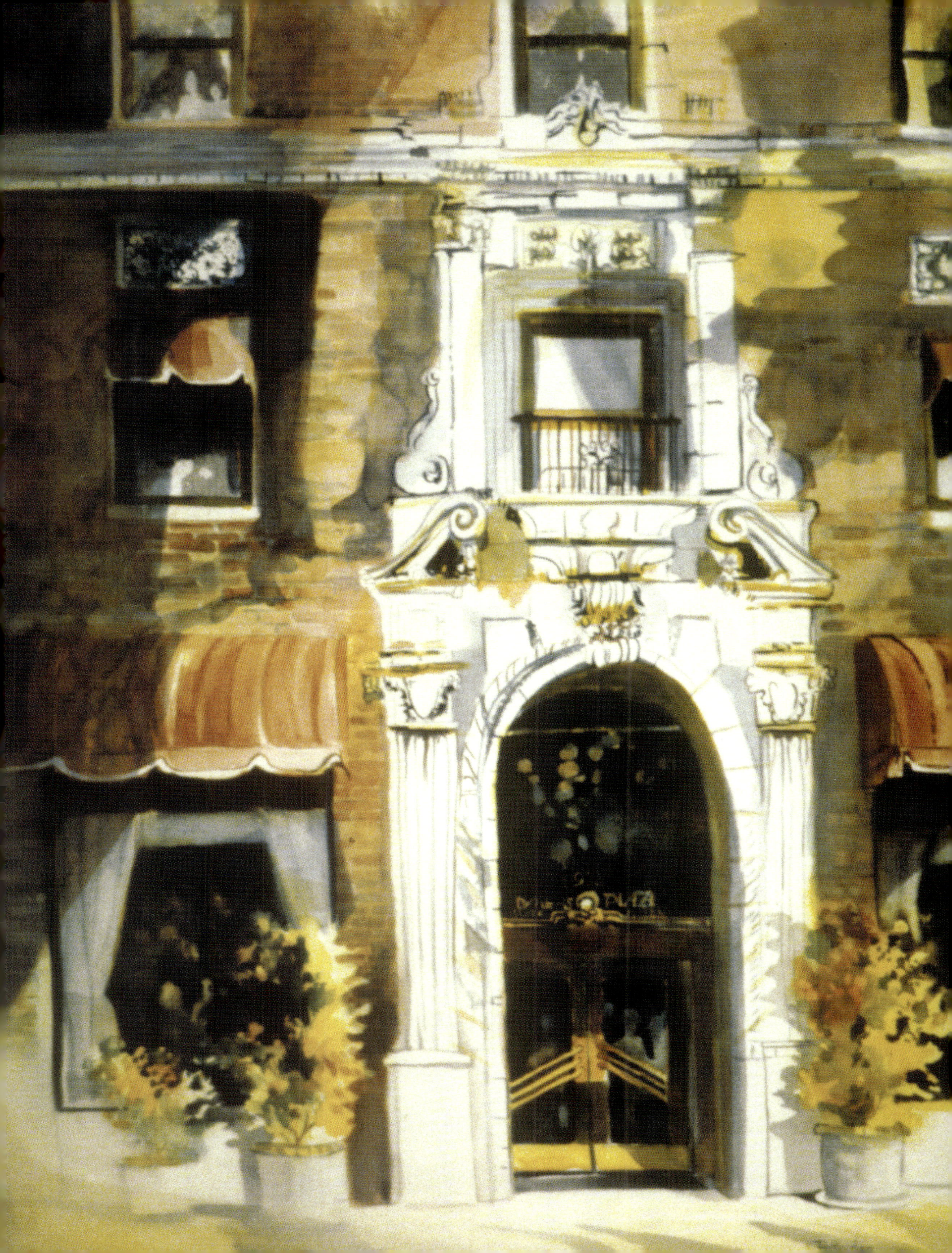

Dallas Plaza Hotel II

watercolor
30x22

View from Harwood Street side.

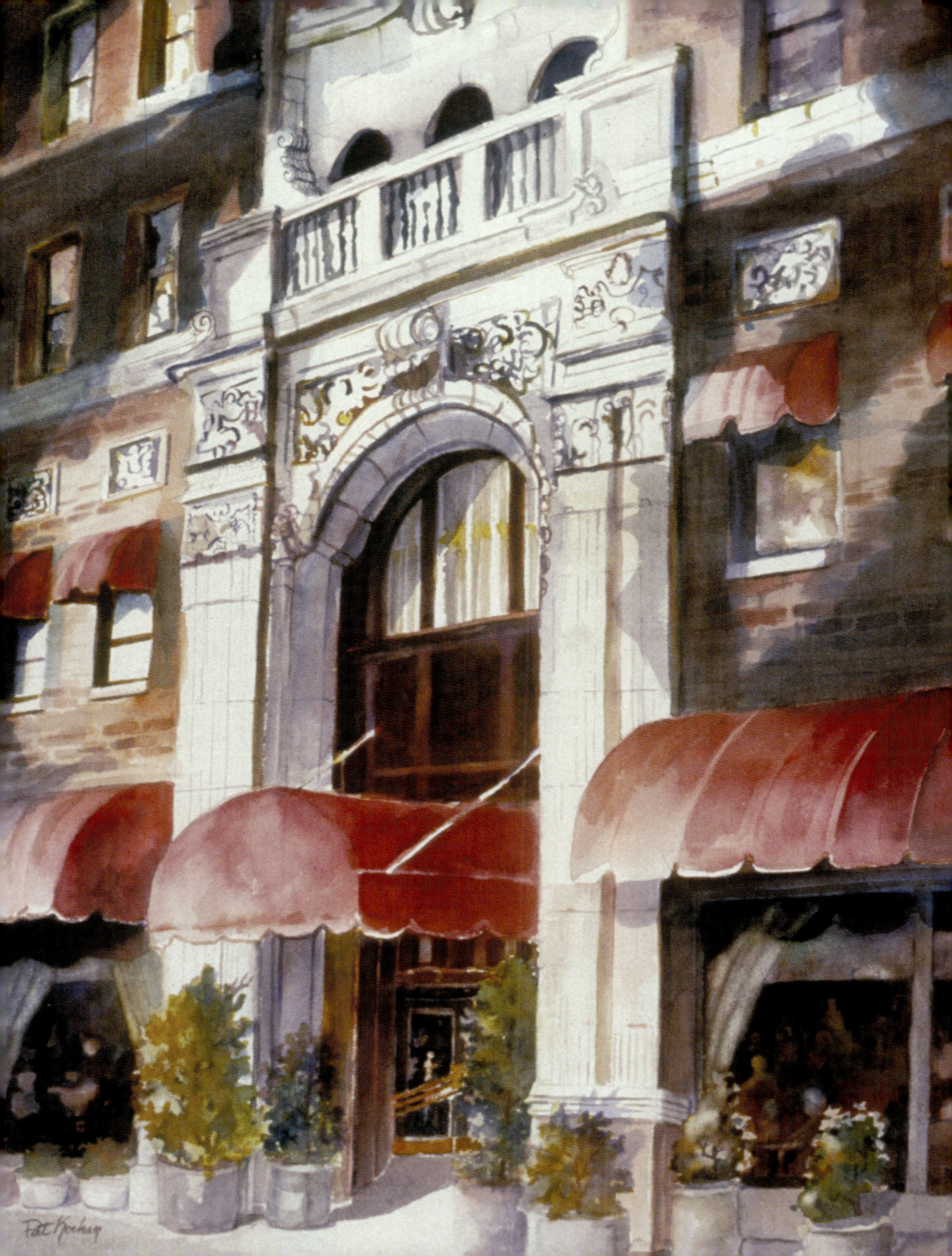

Dallas Plaza Hotel/Lavender

watercolor
30x22

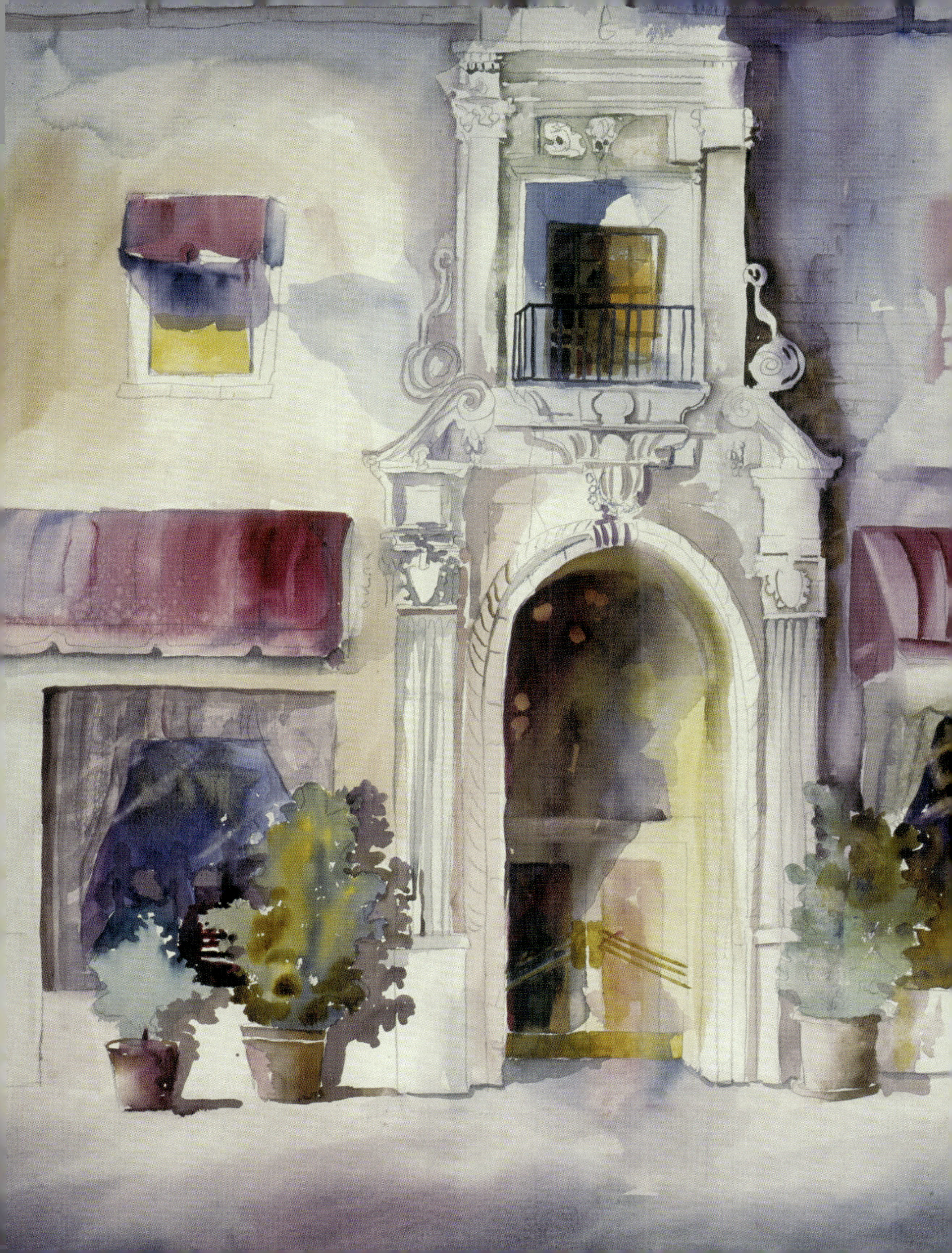

Dallas Tortilla Factory #1

watercolor
22x28

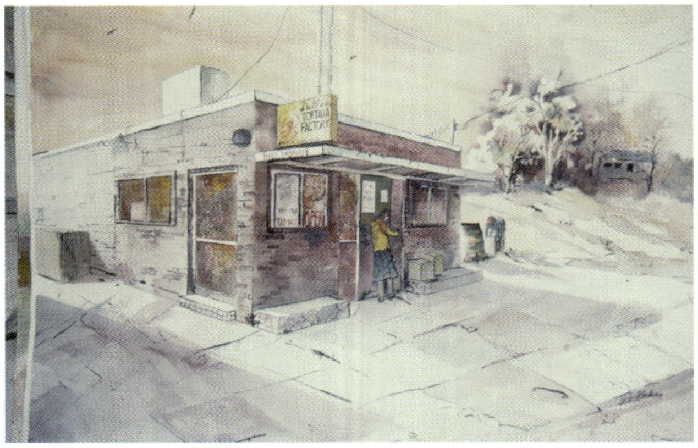

Dallas Tortilla Factory #2

watercolor
22x28

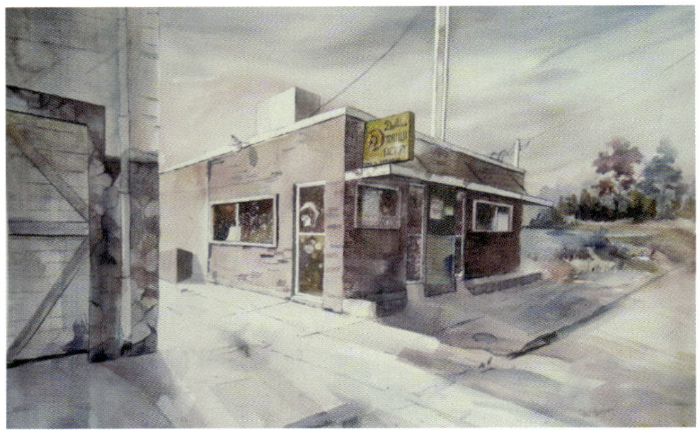

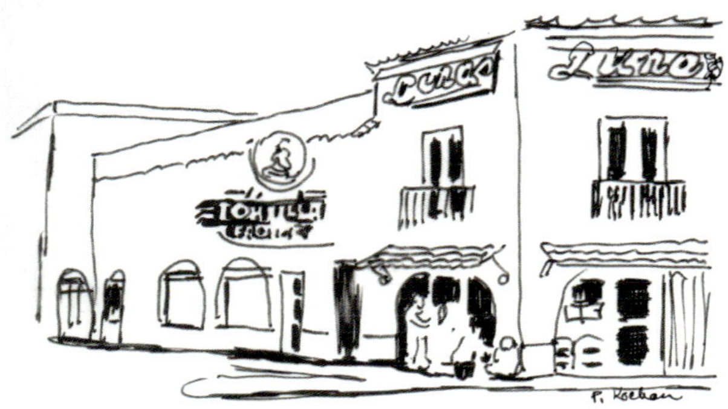

Sketch of Lunas Tortilla Factory

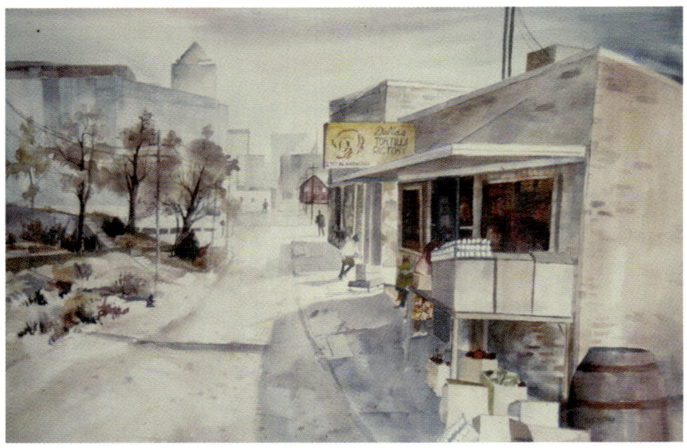

Dallas Tortilla Factory #3

watercolor
22x28

In 1985, Luana Wilsey, an interior designer, commissioned a watercolor painting of the Dallas Tortilla Factory on Harwood Street for the conference room of the Crown Charter National Bank in the Rolex Building at Harwood and Pearl streets. The conference room overlooked the Dallas Tortilla Factory and other small Mexican frame houses and offices of the Mexican community. That area was populated by the Mexican community and was a special legacy for Dallas. Sadly, most of the buildings in that area have been torn down, little by little, and replaced with tall office buildings. A great legacy has been forever lost.

While I was waiting for Luana to pick up the work, I became so interested in the Little Mexico area that I painted about twelve other scenes of the area. Luana was quite excited about these works and gave me a one-woman show in the Rolex Building. I still have pictures, slides, and memories of the area, and I will continue to paint these lost places of Dallas so that future generations may enjoy the memories of them.

My mom would make enchiladas with fresh tortillas she had purchased during a downtown shopping trip from one of the tortilla factories. The factories made fresh tortillas daily. Many Texans love Mexican food and need to have a Mexican meal on a regular basis. Lunas Tortilla Factory is still on McKinney Avenue (as of this writing), and one of my paintings of Lunas hangs in the front room of the business.

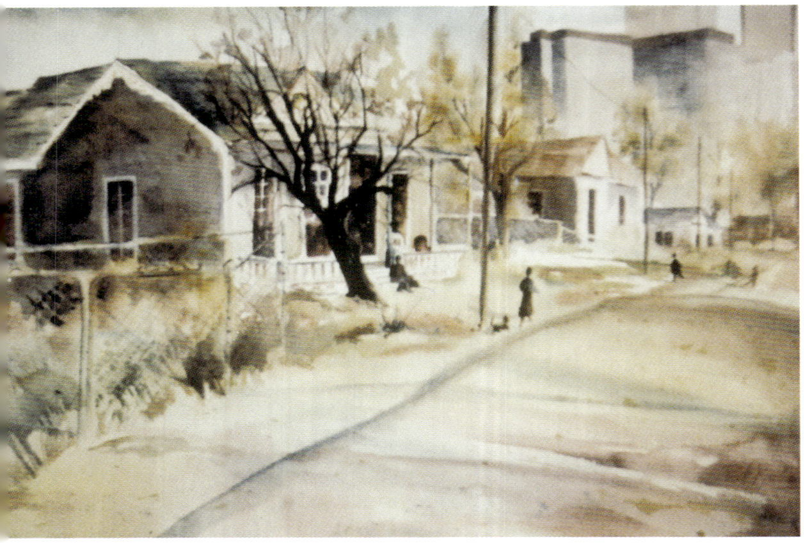

Little Mexico, Harwood Street #1, 2, 3

watercolor
11x15

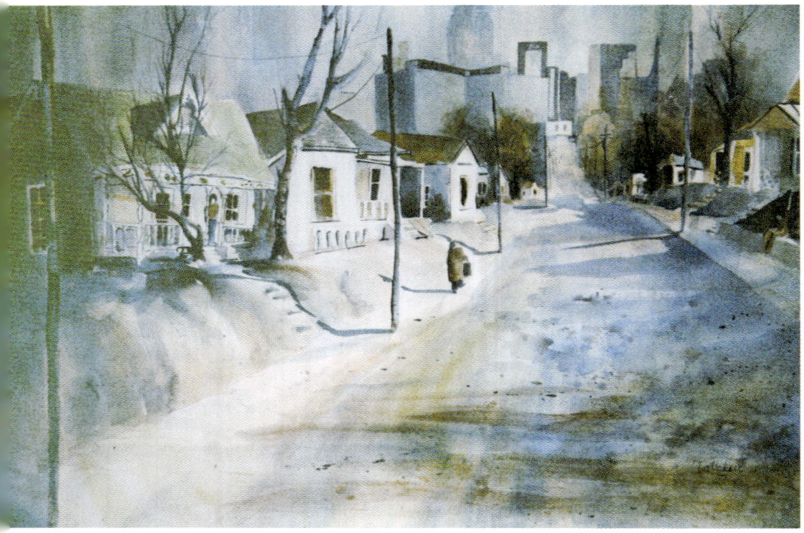

What a shame that Dallas allowed the last of the Little Mexico area of houses to be uprooted. Large office buildings are now in their place. On the right was a lawyer's office; on the left not seen in this painting was a grocery store and bakery called Stados. At the bottom of the hill on the right was the Dallas Tortilla Factory. The building at the end of the street is the Rolex building where I had my first one-woman art show.

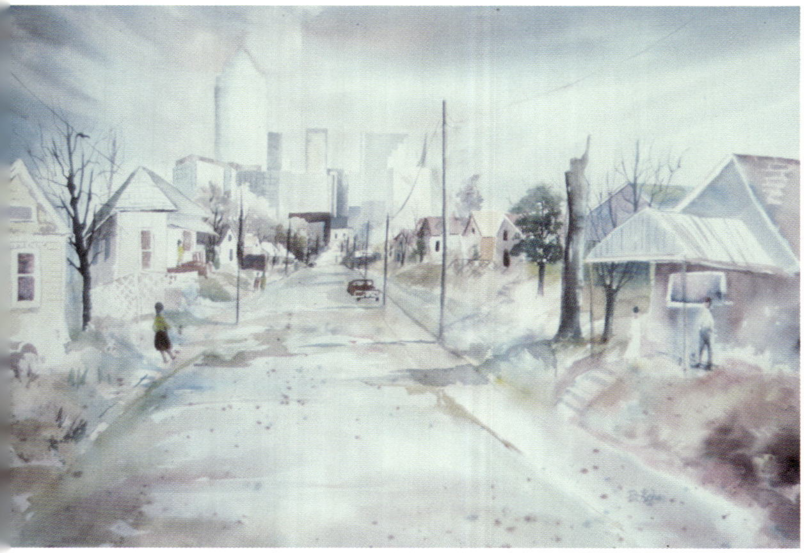

View from Harwood Street

watercolor
15x11

This view of Dallas was from Harwood Street during the 1980s. The First United Methodist Church is nestled below the large buildings of the city.

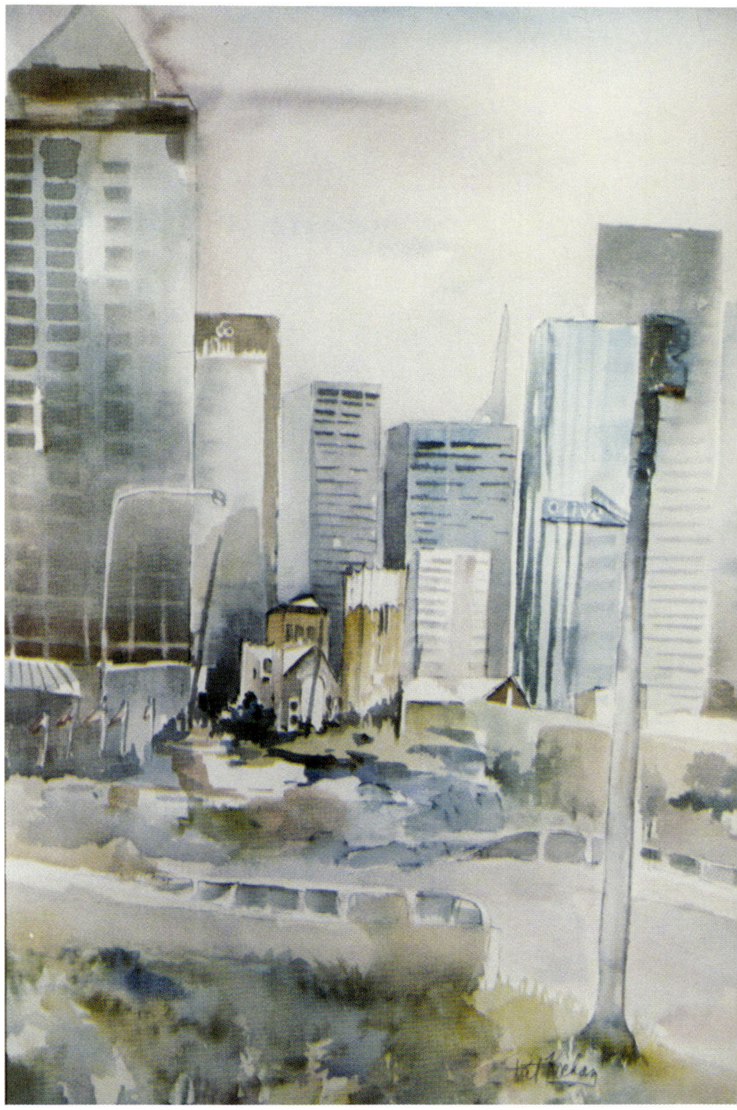

Stados Baking Co.

watercolor
22x30

This little Hispanic baking company was on Harwood Street at the top of the hill behind Channel 13. Large buildings are now replacing this small business.

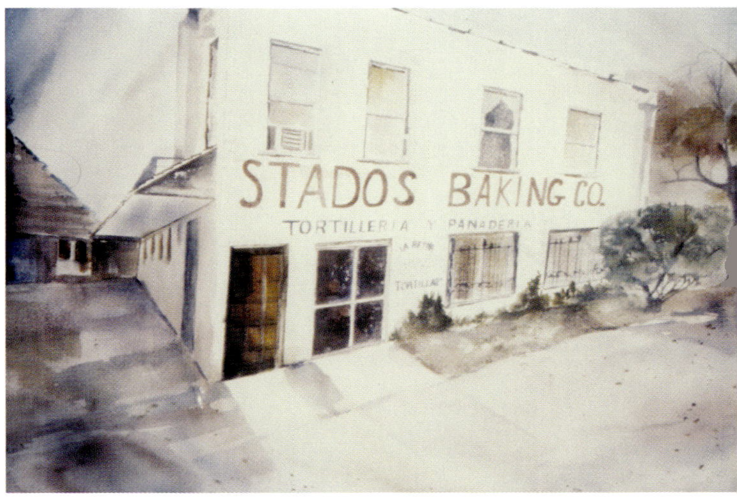

When I was commissioned to paint the Dallas Tortilla Factory, the Crown Charter National Bank also wanted a painting of the initial bank facility, which was the Rolex Building. They purchased both paintings for their collection.

The Rolex Building

watercolor
22x30

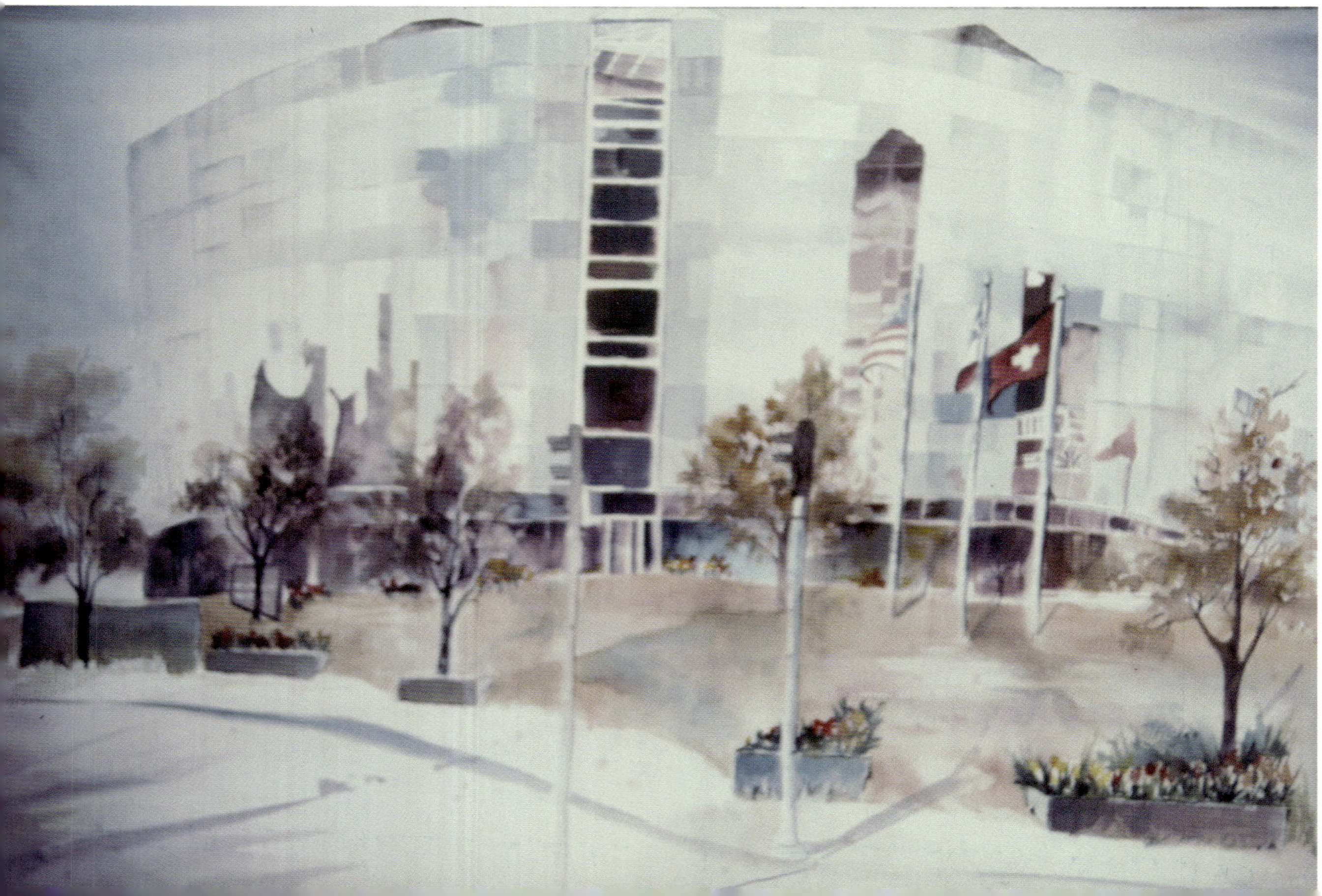

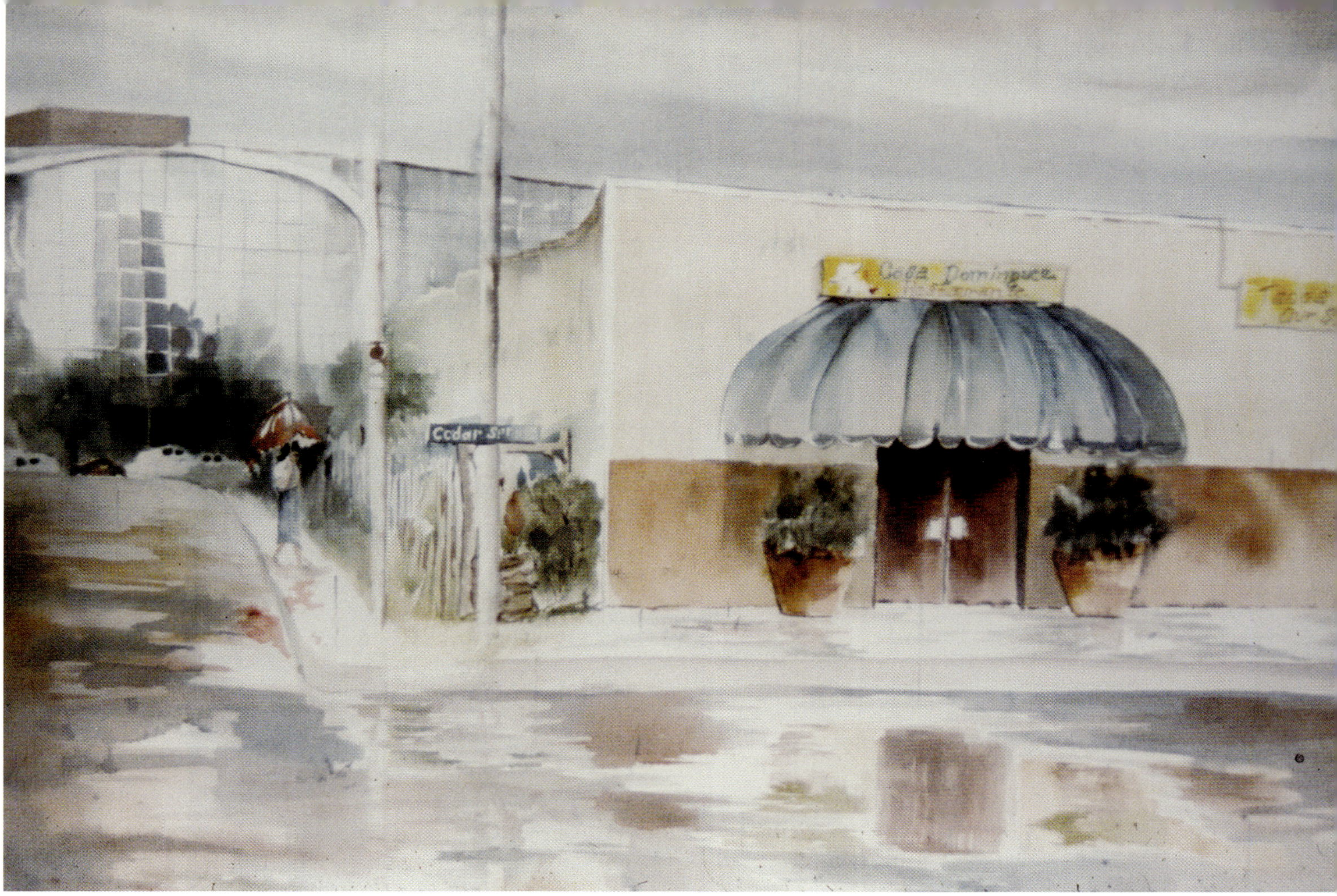

Casa Dominguez #1

watercolor
22x30

The Dominguez family owned this restaurant which was located at Cedar Springs and Pearl Street. The Rolex Building is behind and across the street. Tragically, the restaurant building burned, and this painting burned with it. However, I painted other artworks of the building.

Ratliff's on McKinney Avenue

watercolor
30x22

Ratliff's was an Italian restaurant across the street from El Taxco. It, too, brought people into the city from all over the area. Its Spanish roof and red canopies accentuated the Old World charm of the structure.

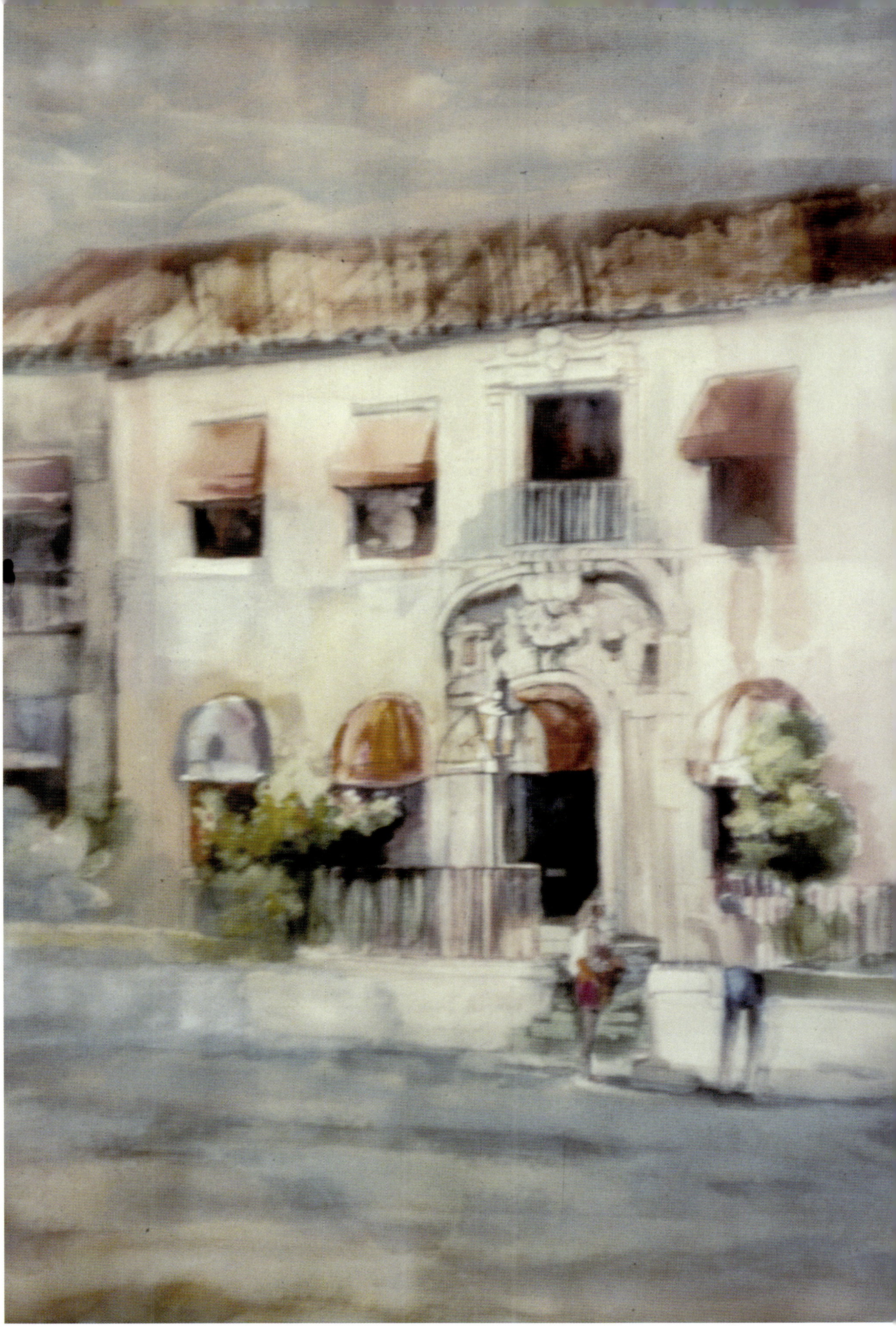

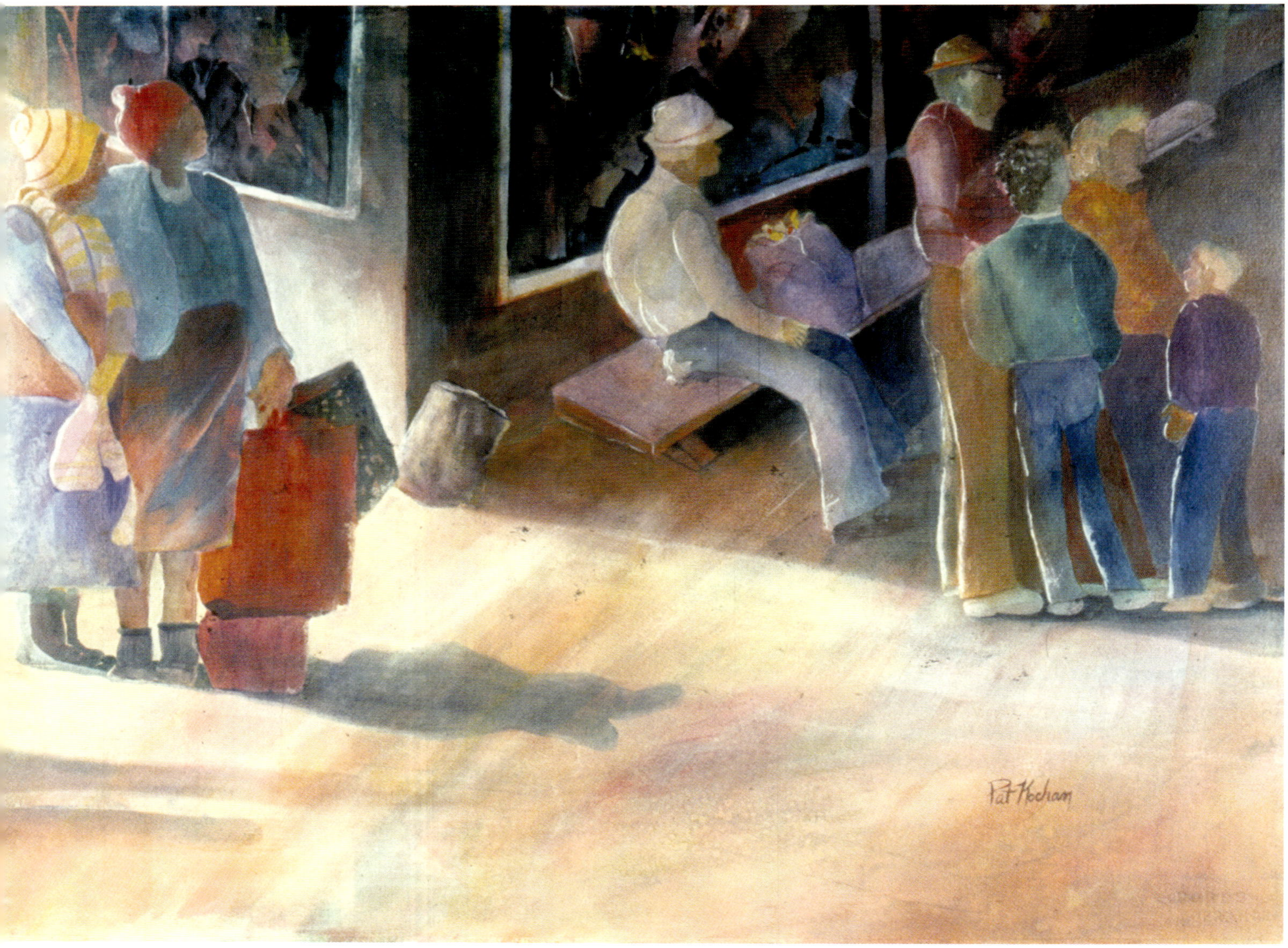

Bus Stop III

acrylic on paper
22x30

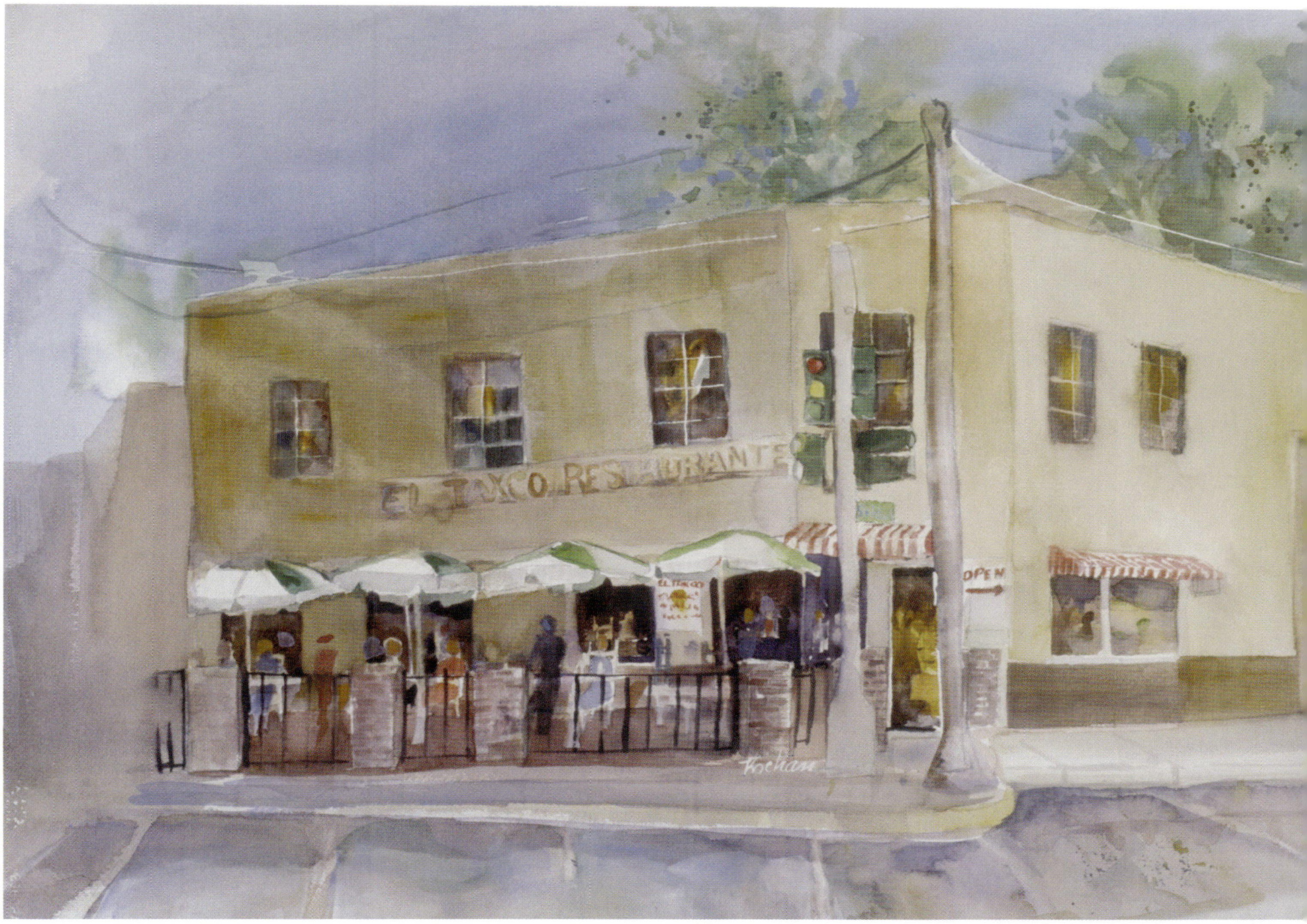

El Taxco #1

watercolor
15x22

The Pete Navarro family had owned this restaurant at the corner of McKinney Avenue and St. Paul Street since the early days of the twentieth century. It was a favorite of people from all parts of Dallas. When I showed Pete a painting of this restaurant, he purchased it on the spot. He never framed it; he just stuck it on the wall along with family pictures. After Pete died, the family started another restaurant in North Dallas, called Casa Navarro.

El Taxco/Warm

watercolor
30x22

I painted several views of this restaurant. I enjoy painting people eating, drinking, and being merry. I enjoy watching their gestures and studying the personalities.

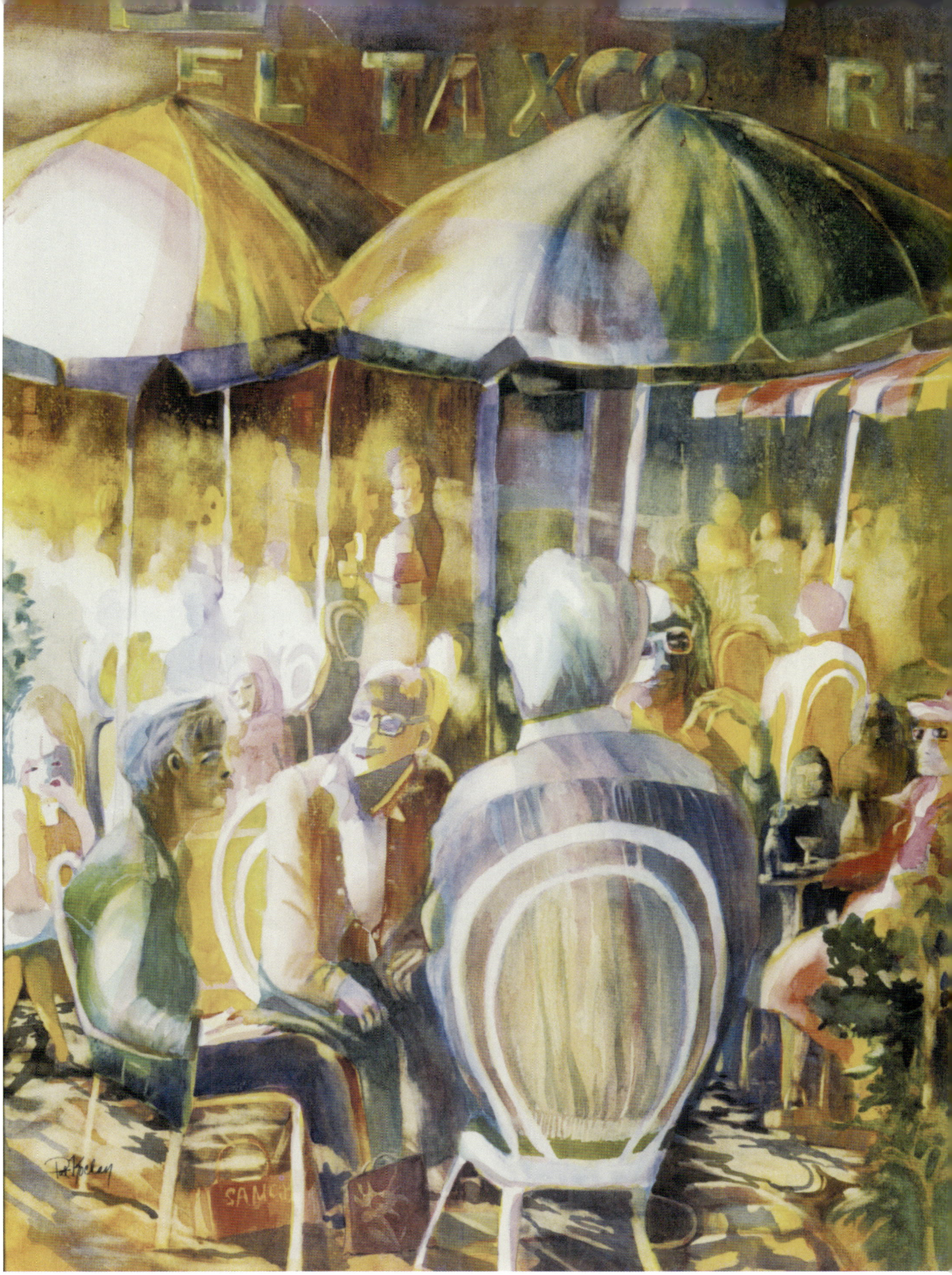
EL TAXCO RE

El Taxco/Cool

watercolor
30x22

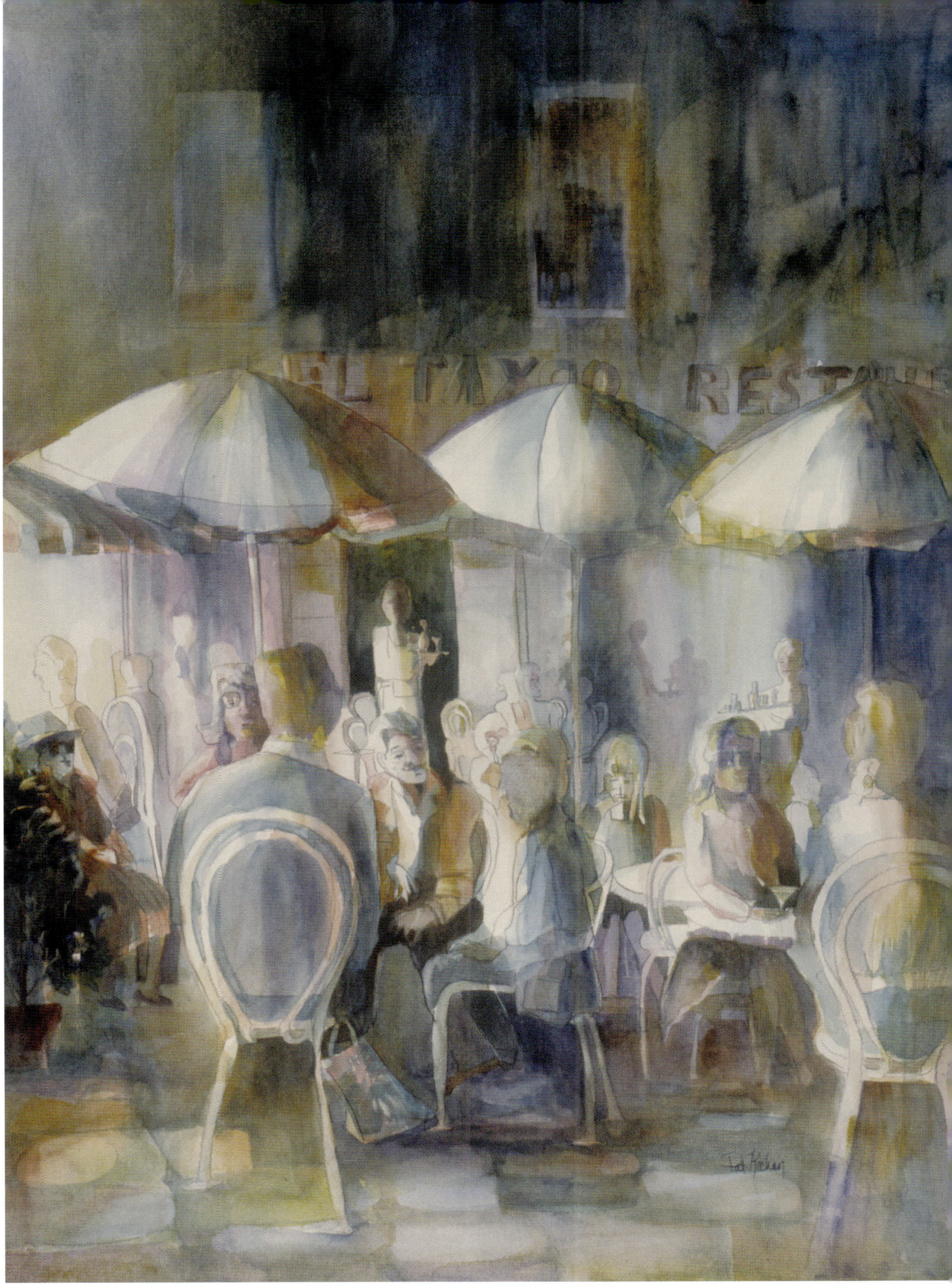

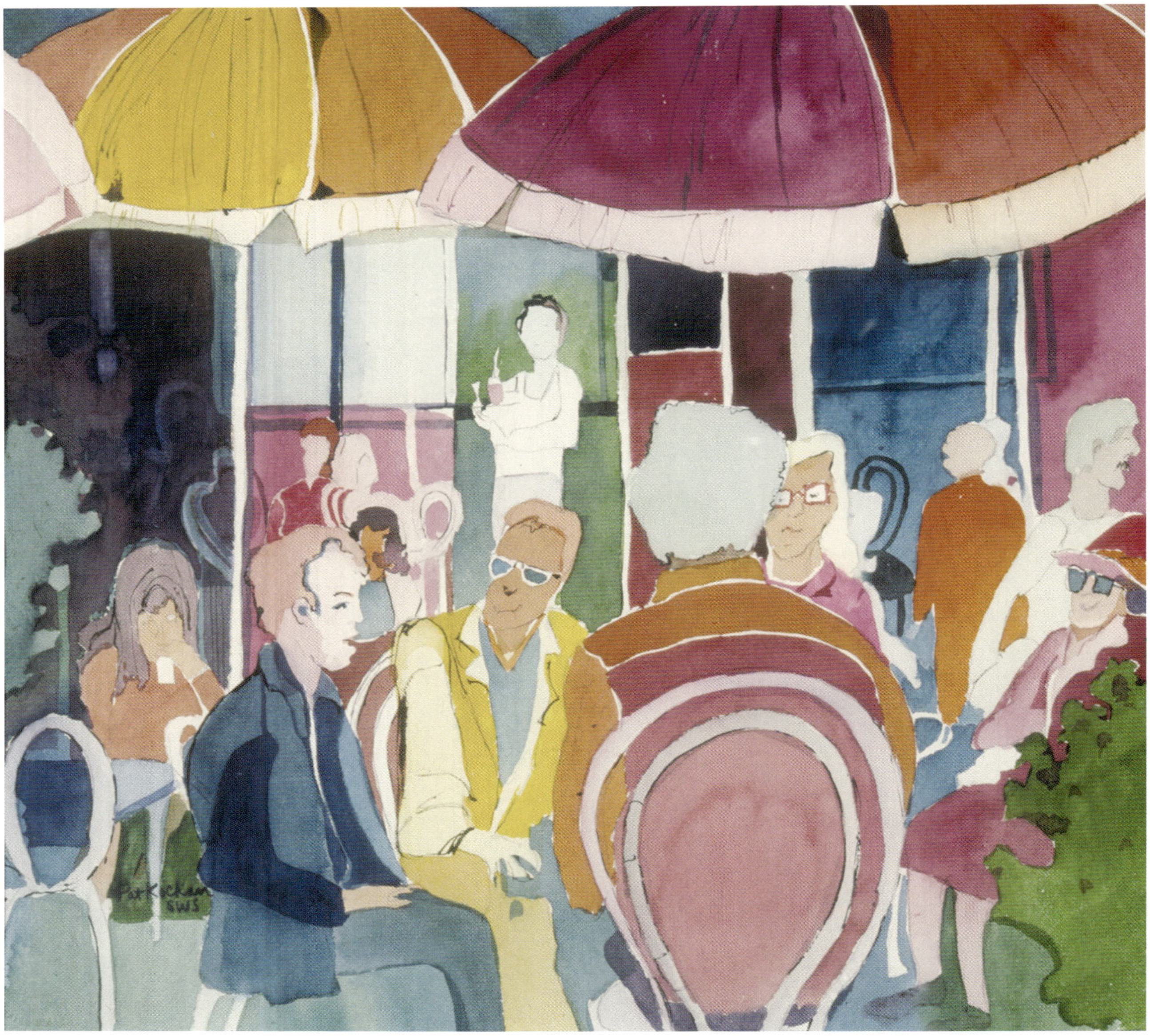

El Taxco/Color

watercolor
14x15

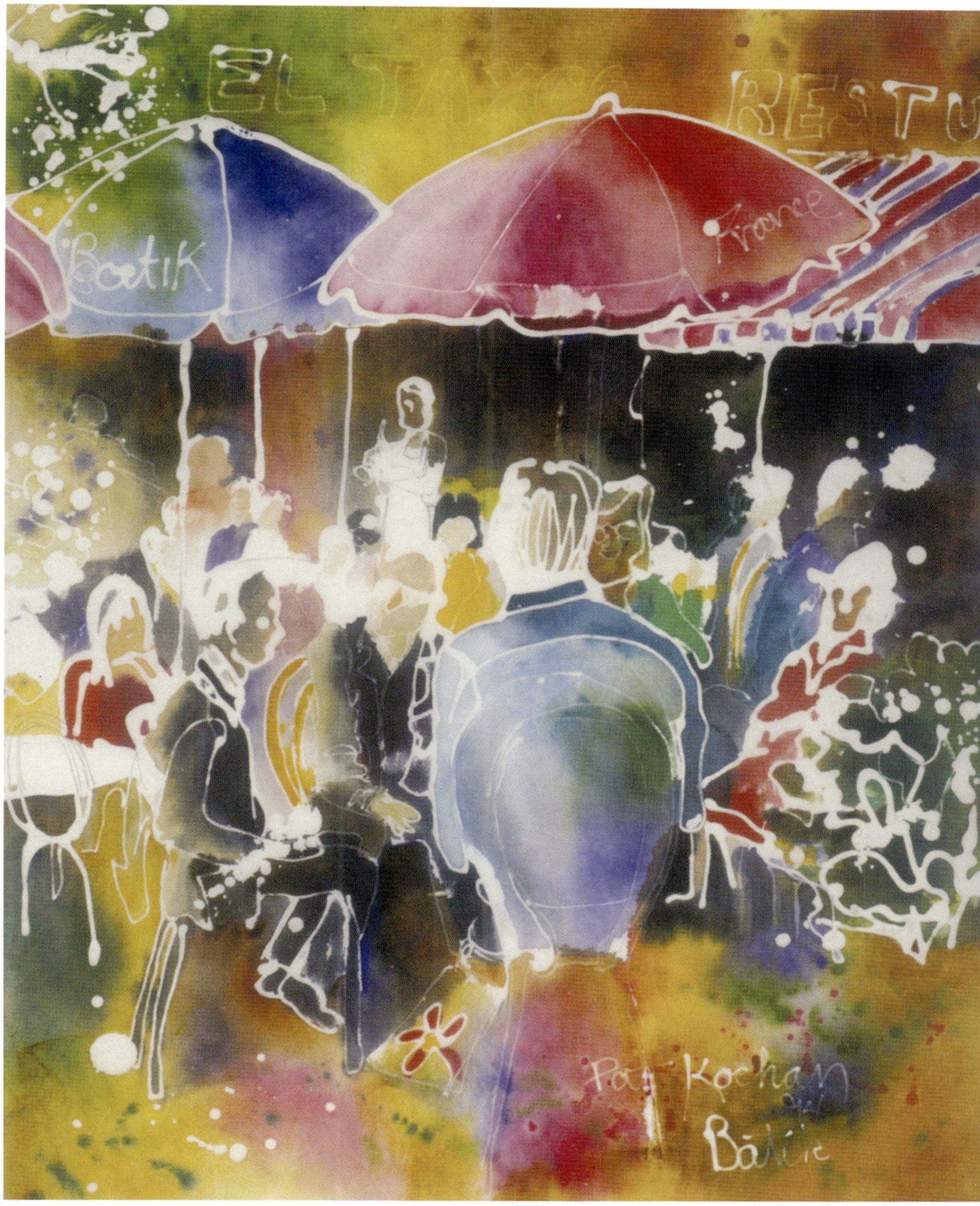

El Taxco/Batik

batik
22x24

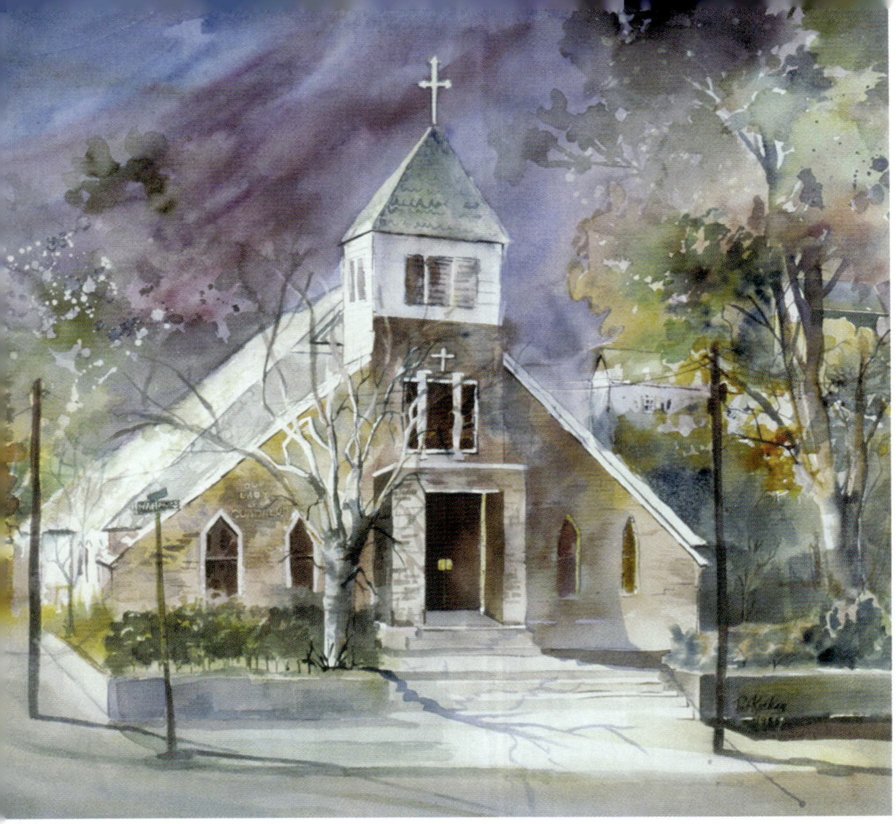

Our Lady of Guadalupe Church was next to St. Anne's Catholic School at Caroline and Harwood streets. In its early days, the church was the center for all of the important activities of the Mexican population. After years of deterioration, a new church was built on Ross Avenue. The old structure burned a few years after this painting was completed.

Our Lady of Guadalupe Church

watercolor
24x24

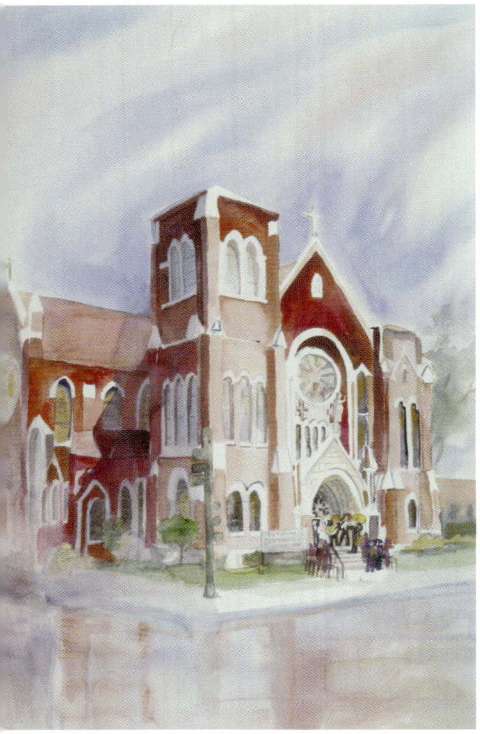

Cathedral Guadalupe Catholic Church

watercolor
22x30

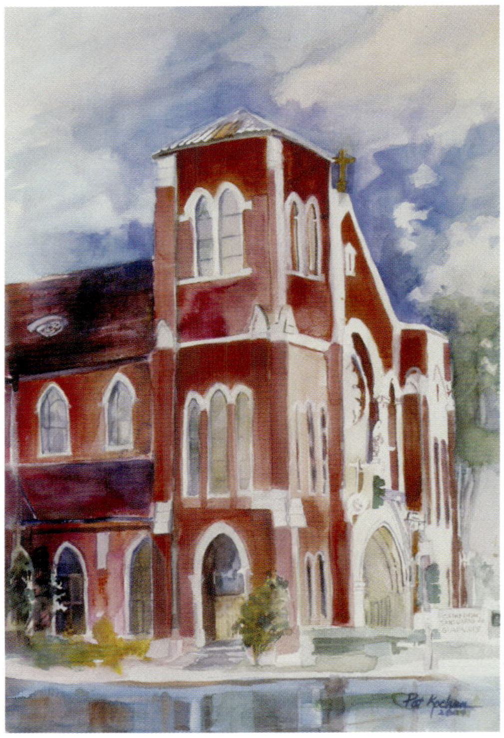

This is the center of the Mexican-American Community of Dallas. The view from the street looking into the church is phenomenal. It is not unusual to see a street full of people going into this church. It is a Dallas landmark to be cherished.

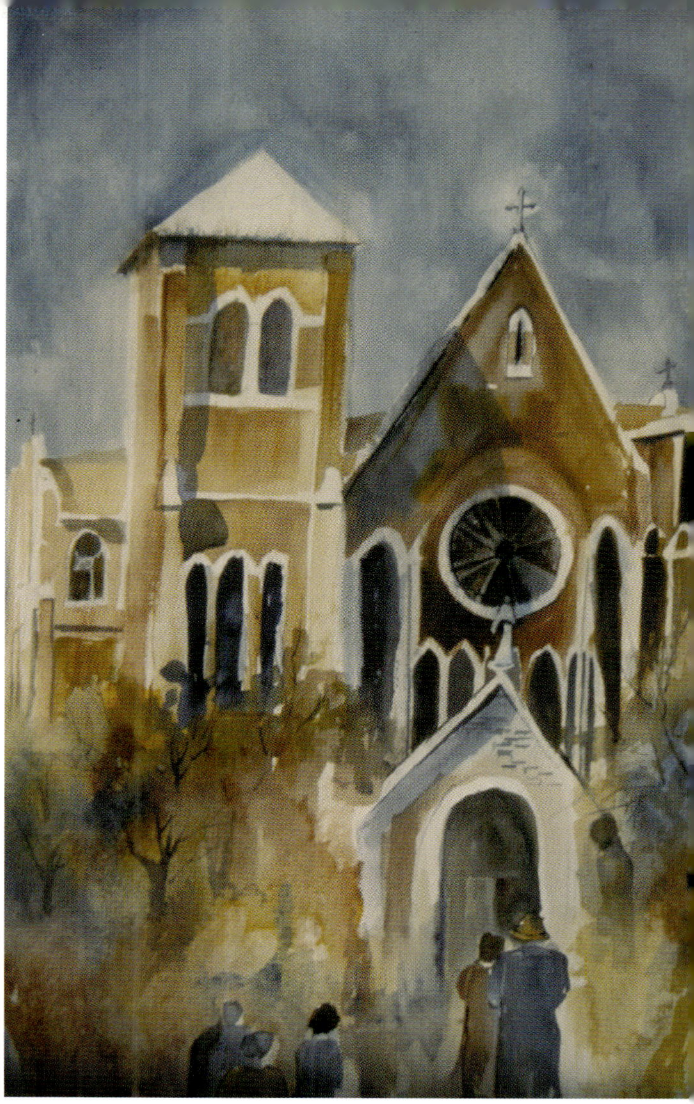

Cathedral Guadalupe Catholic Church

watercolor
28x22

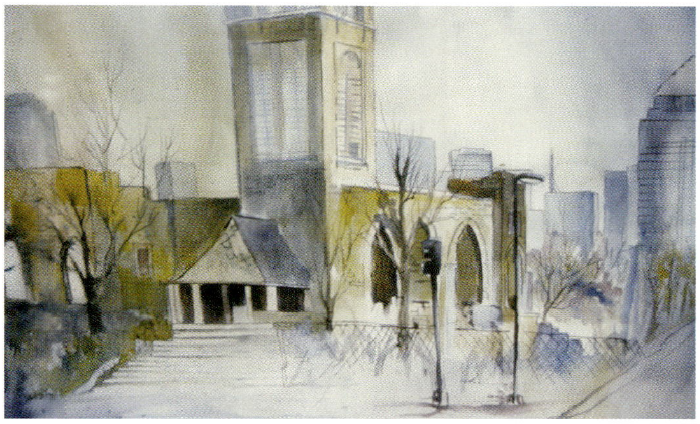

Church on McKinney Avenue

watercolor
24x24

I never knew what happened to this church (or its denomination) or why it burned. This was the structure left from the ruin. The church was on the corner across the street from the building now called the Crescent.

Center of All

watercolor
30x40

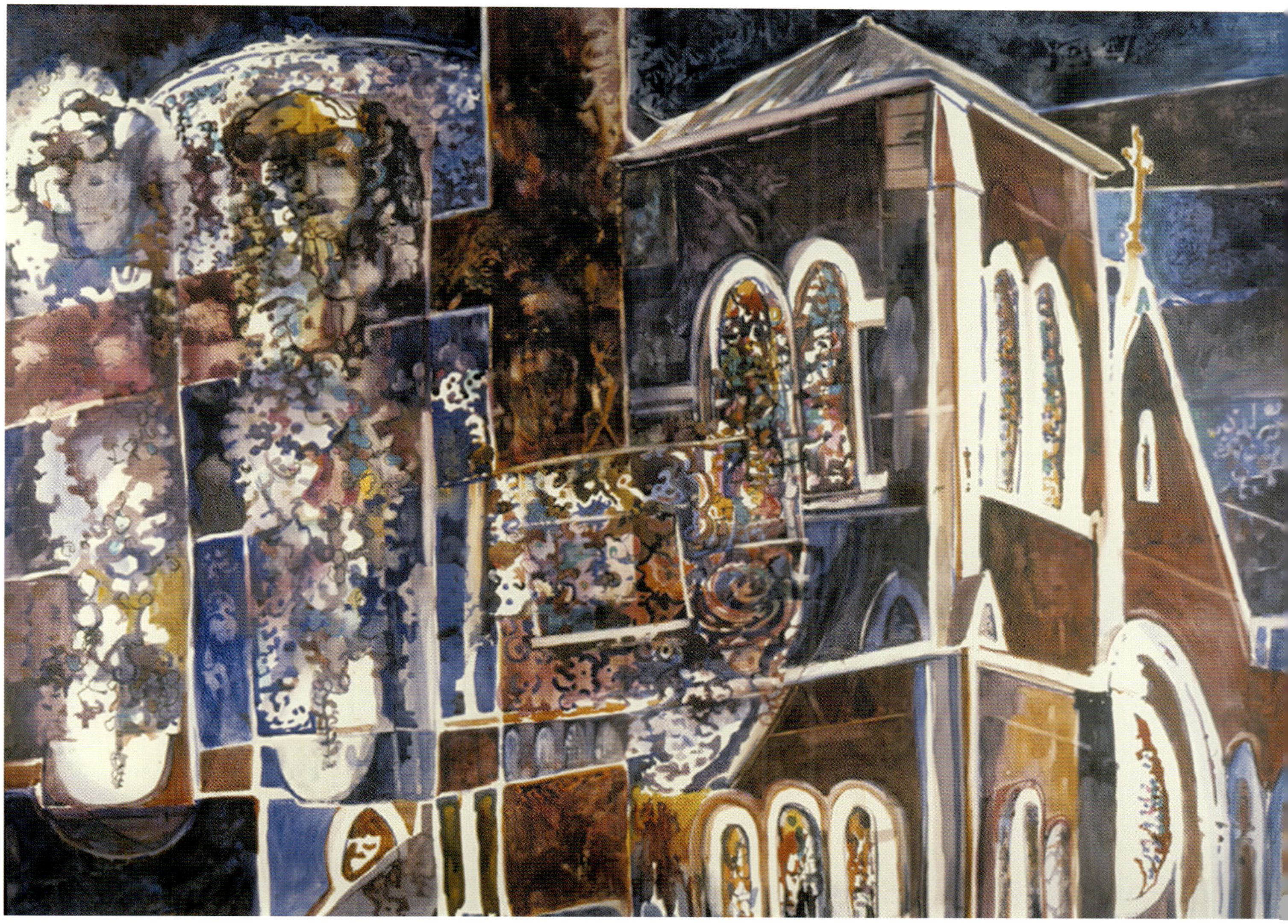

Mercantile against the New

watercolor/acrylic/gouache
48x28

The smaller bank building on the left with the clock on its steeple is the Mercantile National Bank building at Main and Ervay streets. Built in 1942, this thirty-six-story building was once the tallest in the state. The building on the right changed to Bank One.

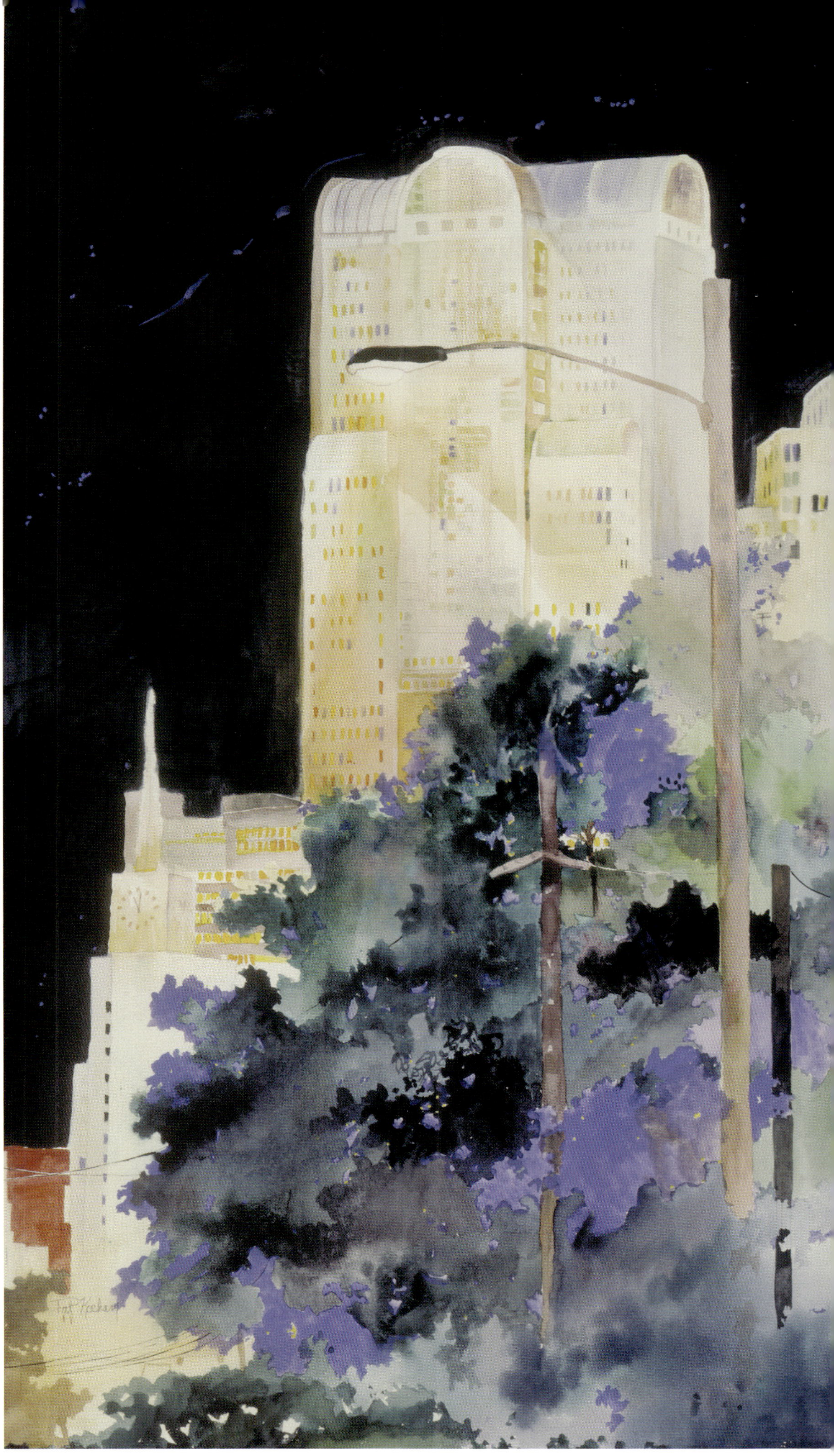

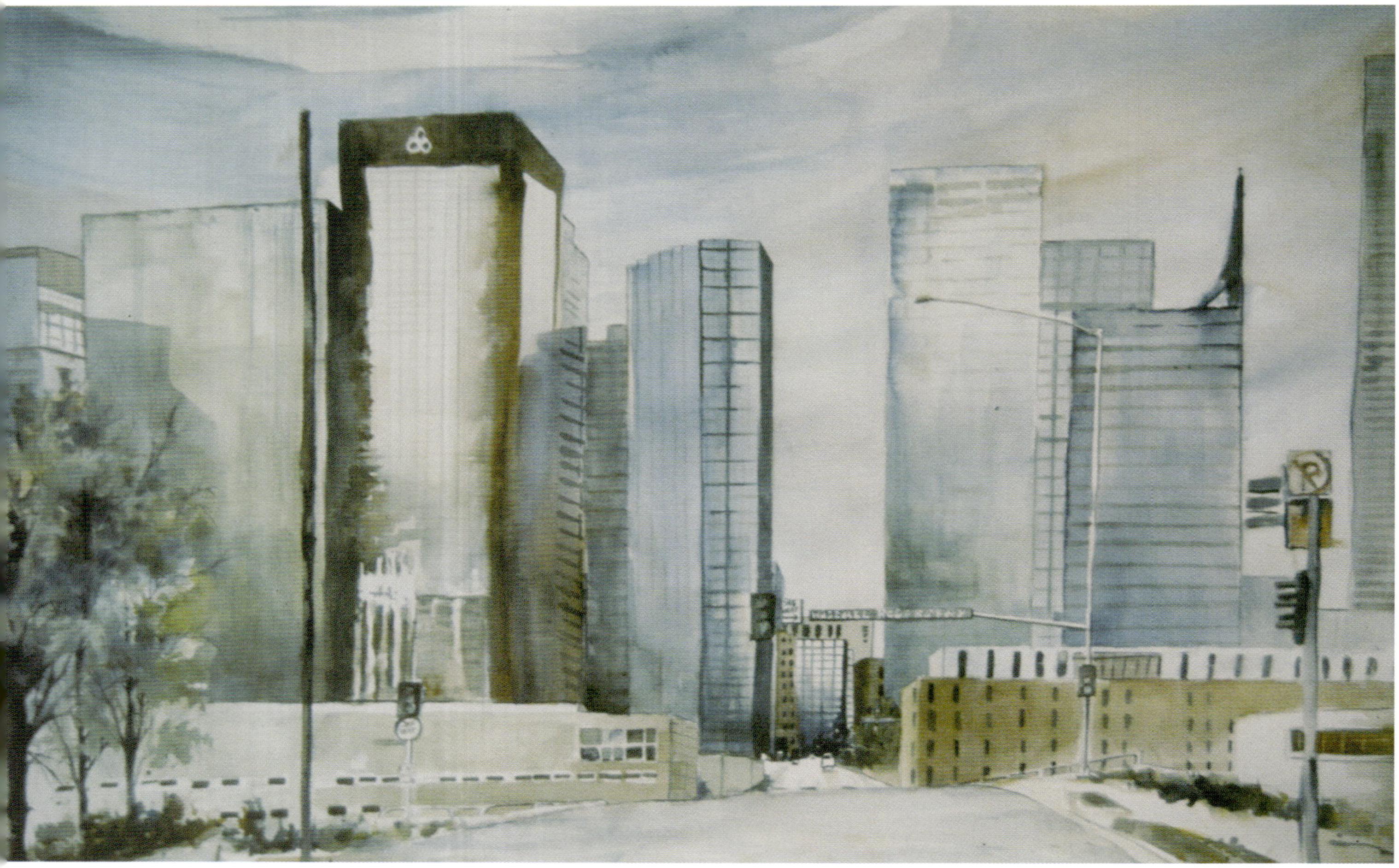

Skyline View from Harwood Street

watercolor
22x30

Skyline View from Olive Street

watercolor
22x30

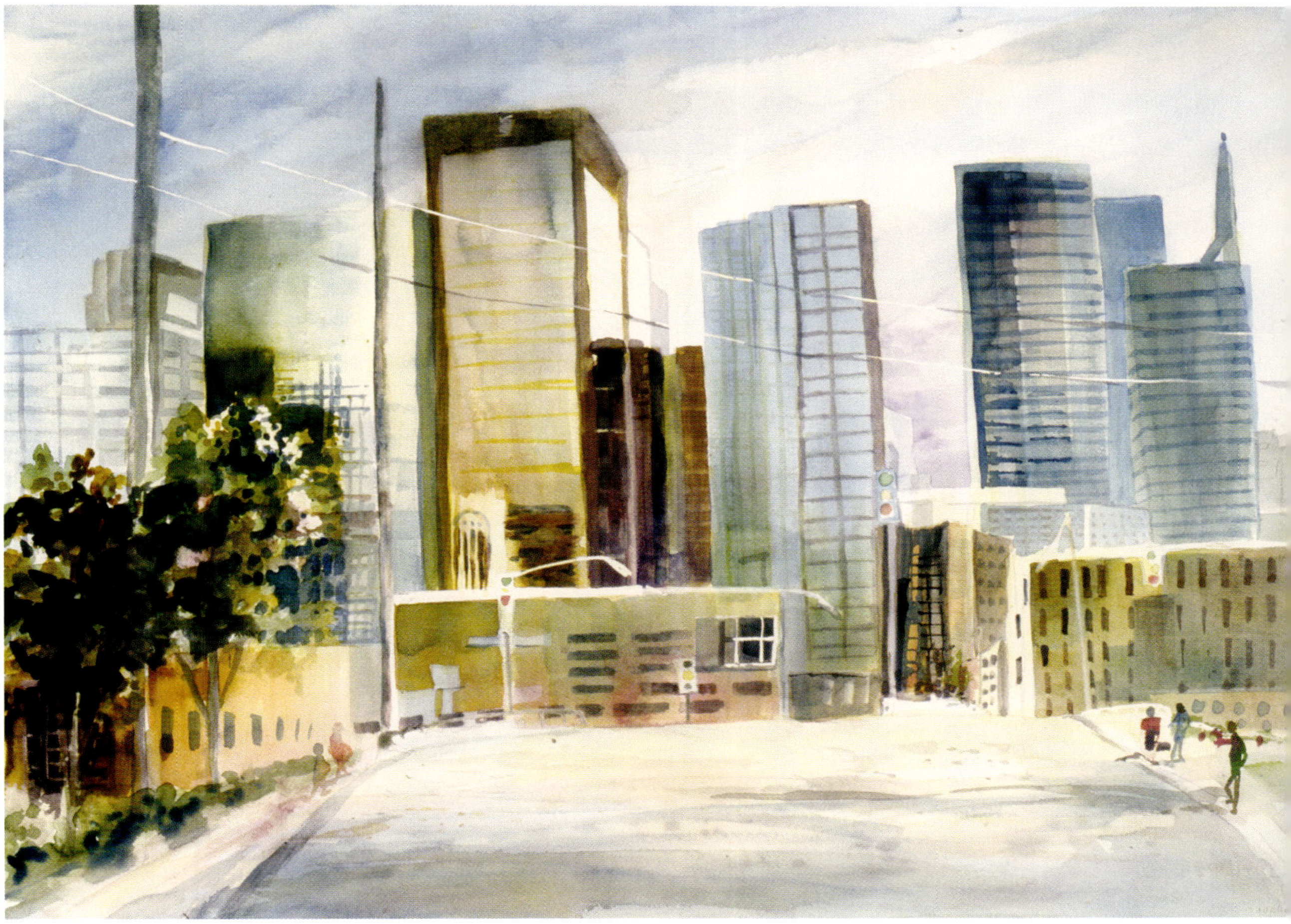

Forty-Two Stories

watercolor
22x30

In the '90s, my husband John and I attended a wedding in the Petroleum Club on the forty-second floor. What a view! I did not have a camera with me on that occasion, but I went to the studio the next day and painted this amazing site from memory.

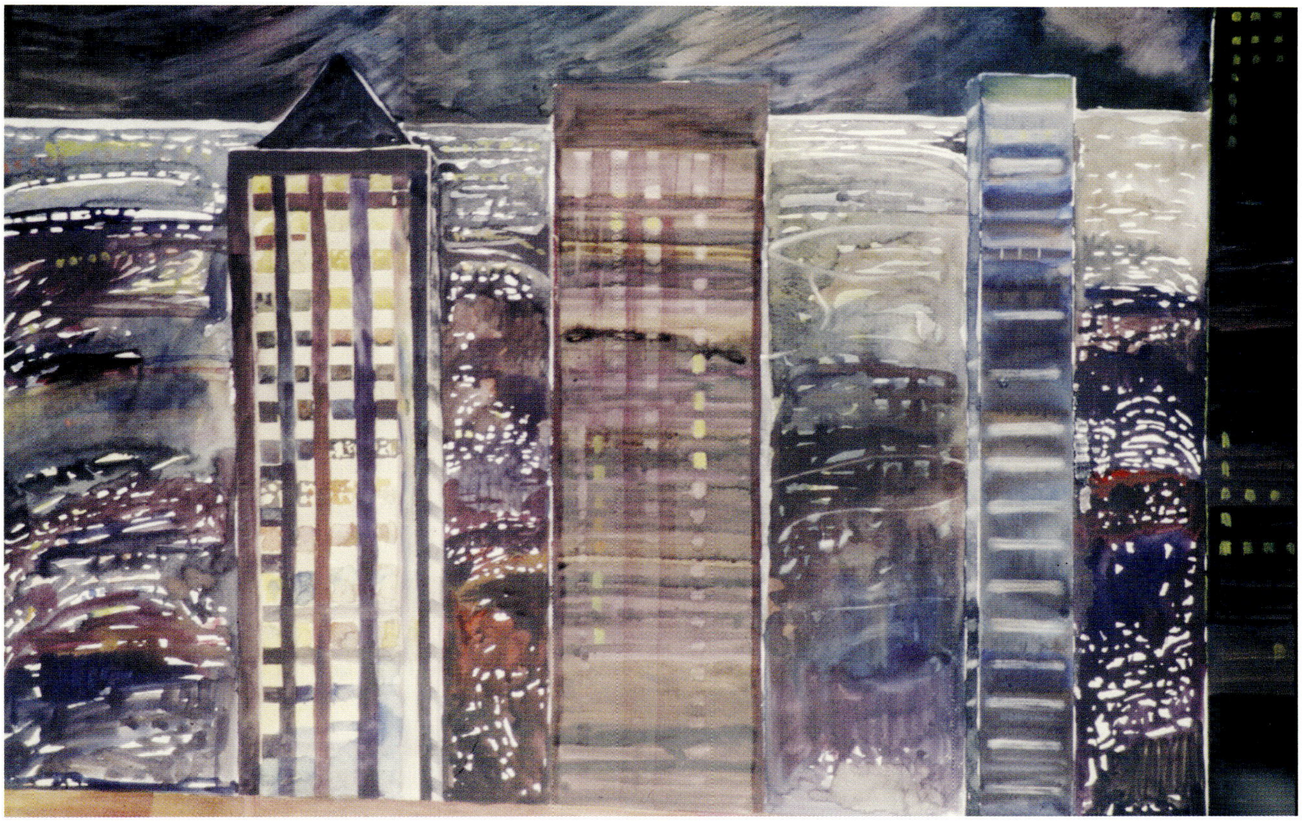

Under the Freeway

acrylic on canvas
30x30

Many people become street people due to bad luck, such as loss of jobs or other problems too numerous to mention. I became aware of what a terrible problem this is when I spent time downtown, sketching and taking pictures for this series of paintings. I saw people sleeping in boxes, in the cold under the overpasses, or wherever they could find shelter. This painting is symbolic of that time when our city tried to ignore these people. Shelters were finally built for many of them, but the number of homeless continues to grow.

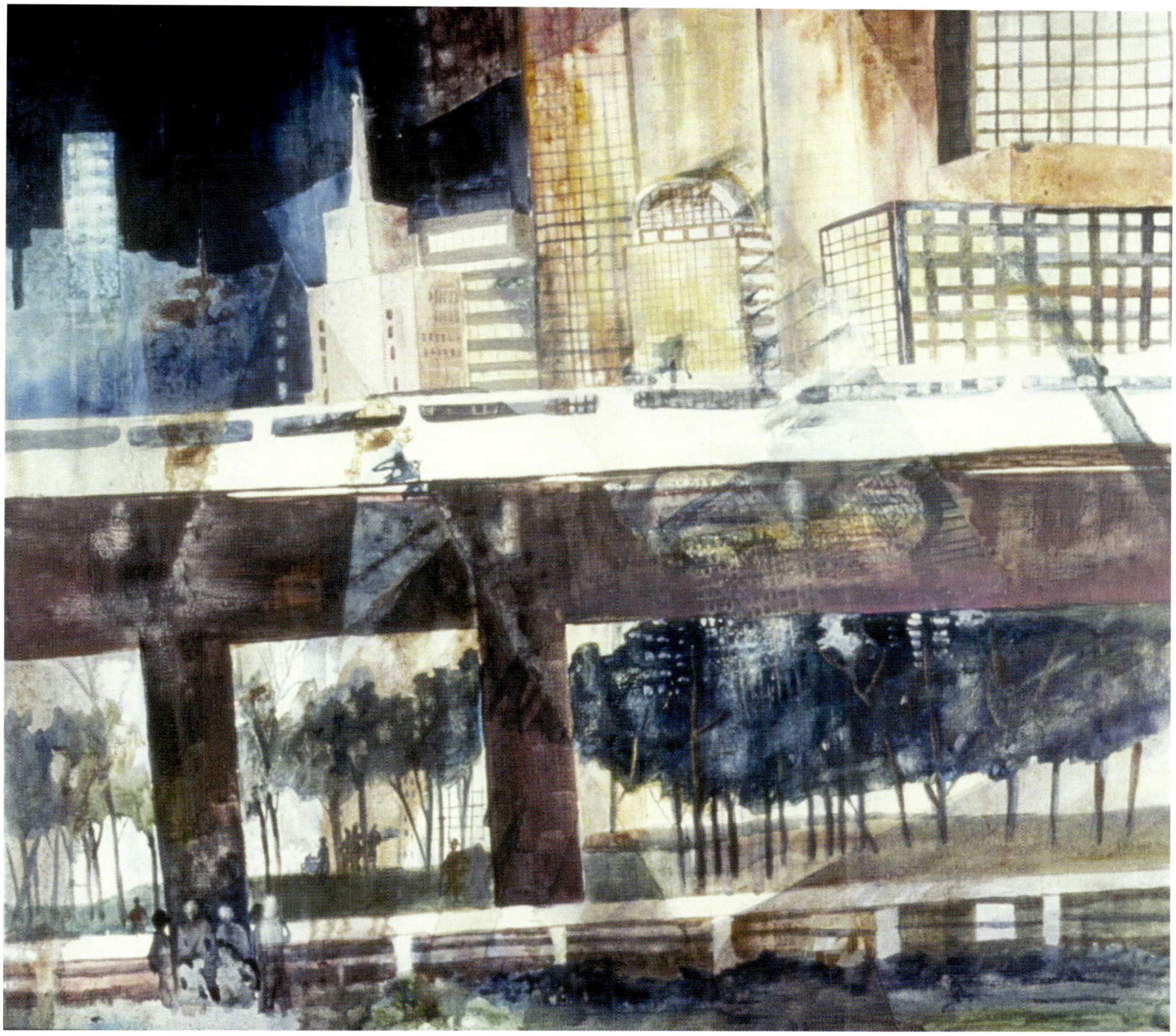

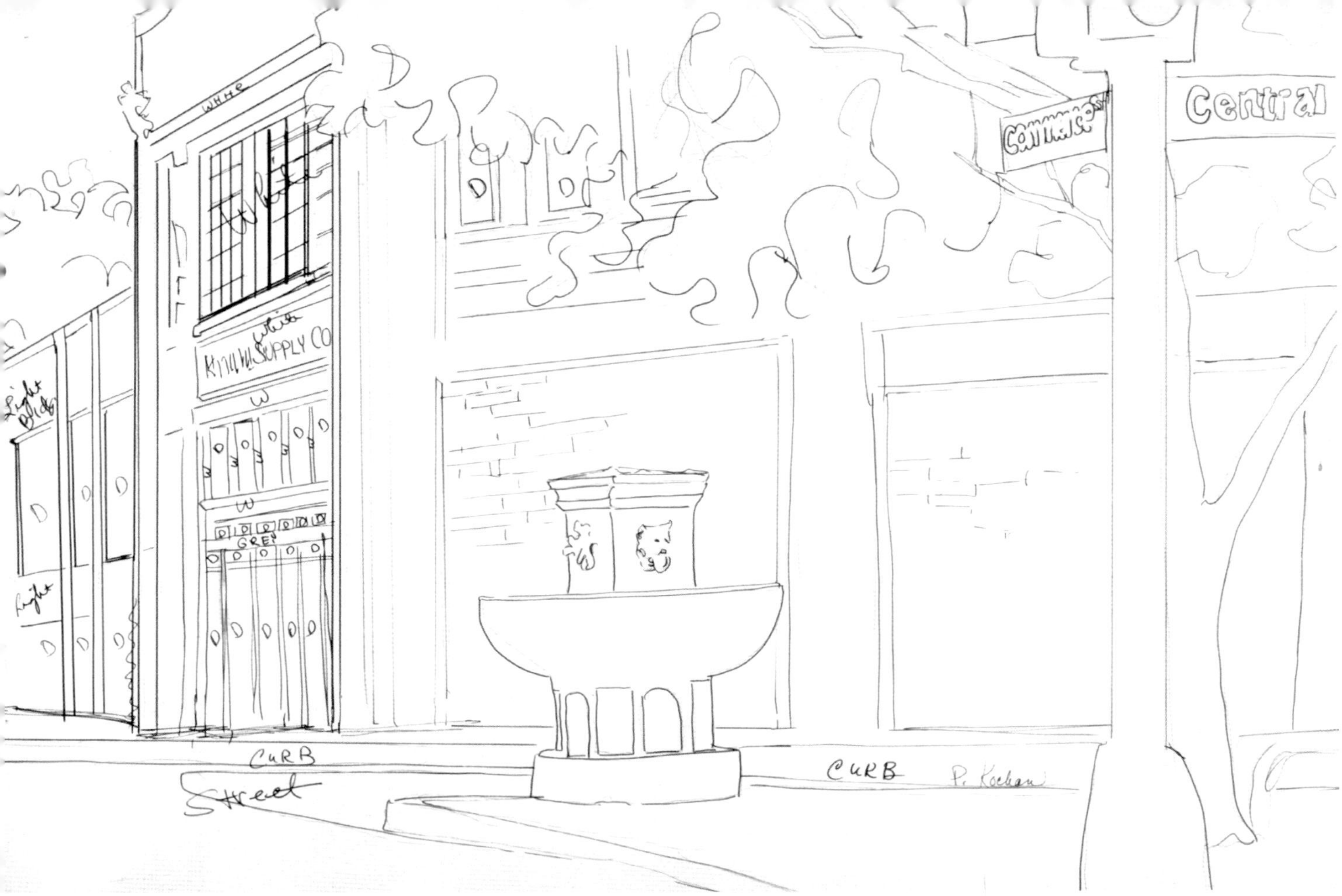

Sketch of Horse Trough

ink
28x30

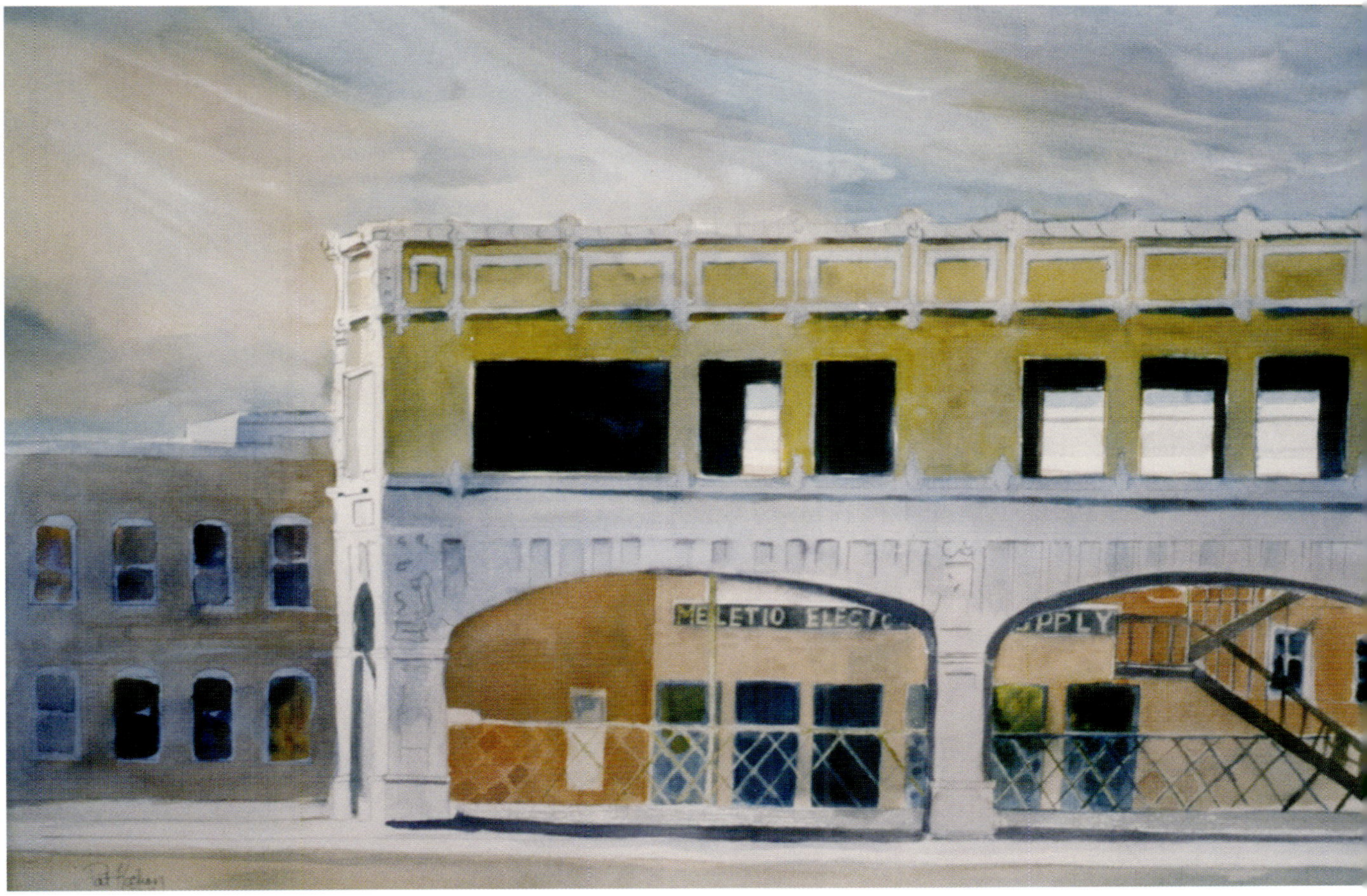

Dallas Landmark

watercolor
28x30

This building has such an interesting shape. At one time, it housed the KRLD Radio Station. I was especially drawn to the horse trough in the middle of the brick street to the left of this building. It was given to the city from France. Meletio Electric Supply Co. is in the rear.

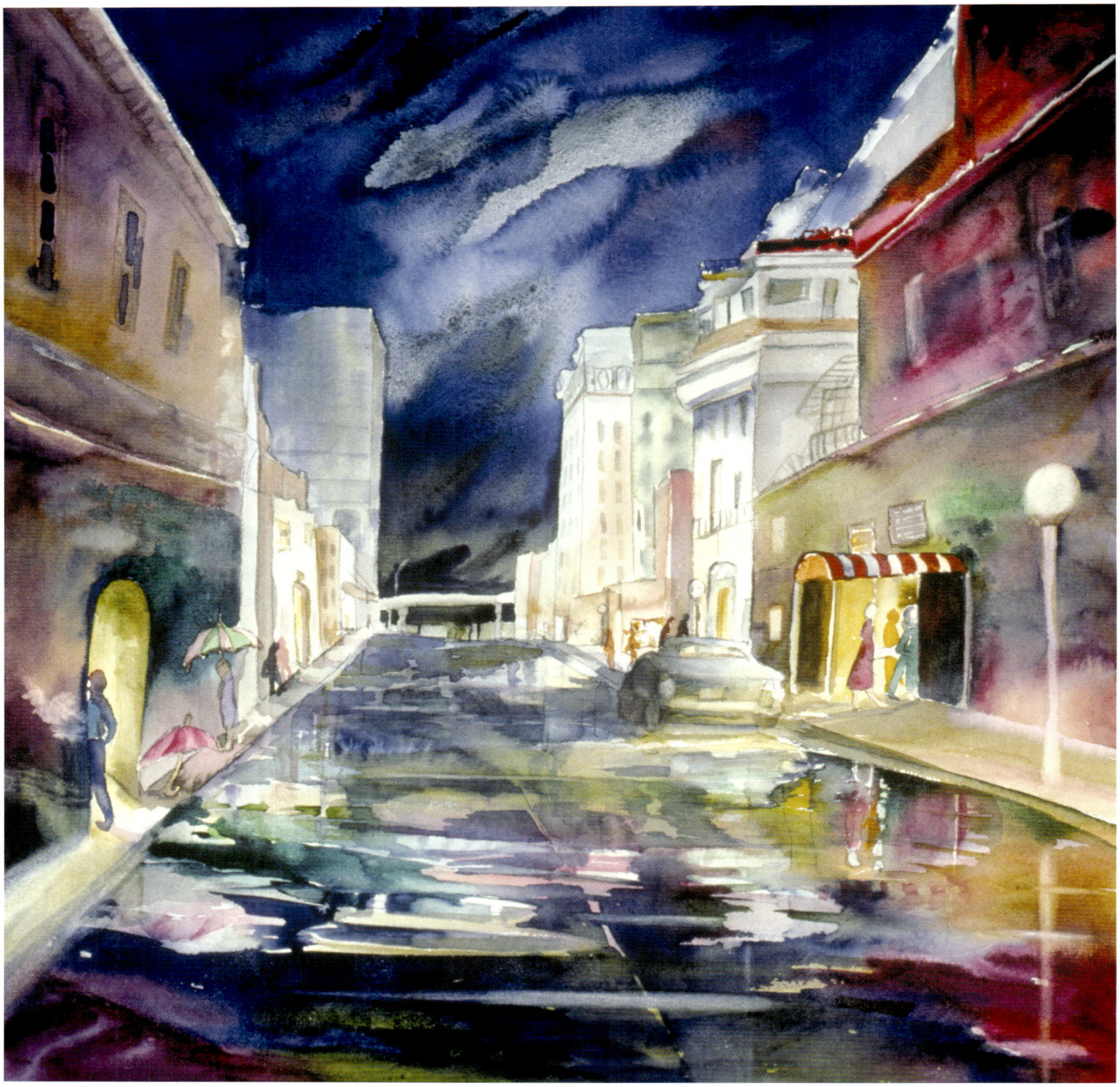

Slick Street

watercolor
22x22

I painted this piece in 1998, strictly from my memory of the Municipal Building on the right, and I dreamed up some buildings to put around it. The bridge at the end of the street represents Central Expressway. I wanted to show the beautiful, colorful reflections we see when it rains.

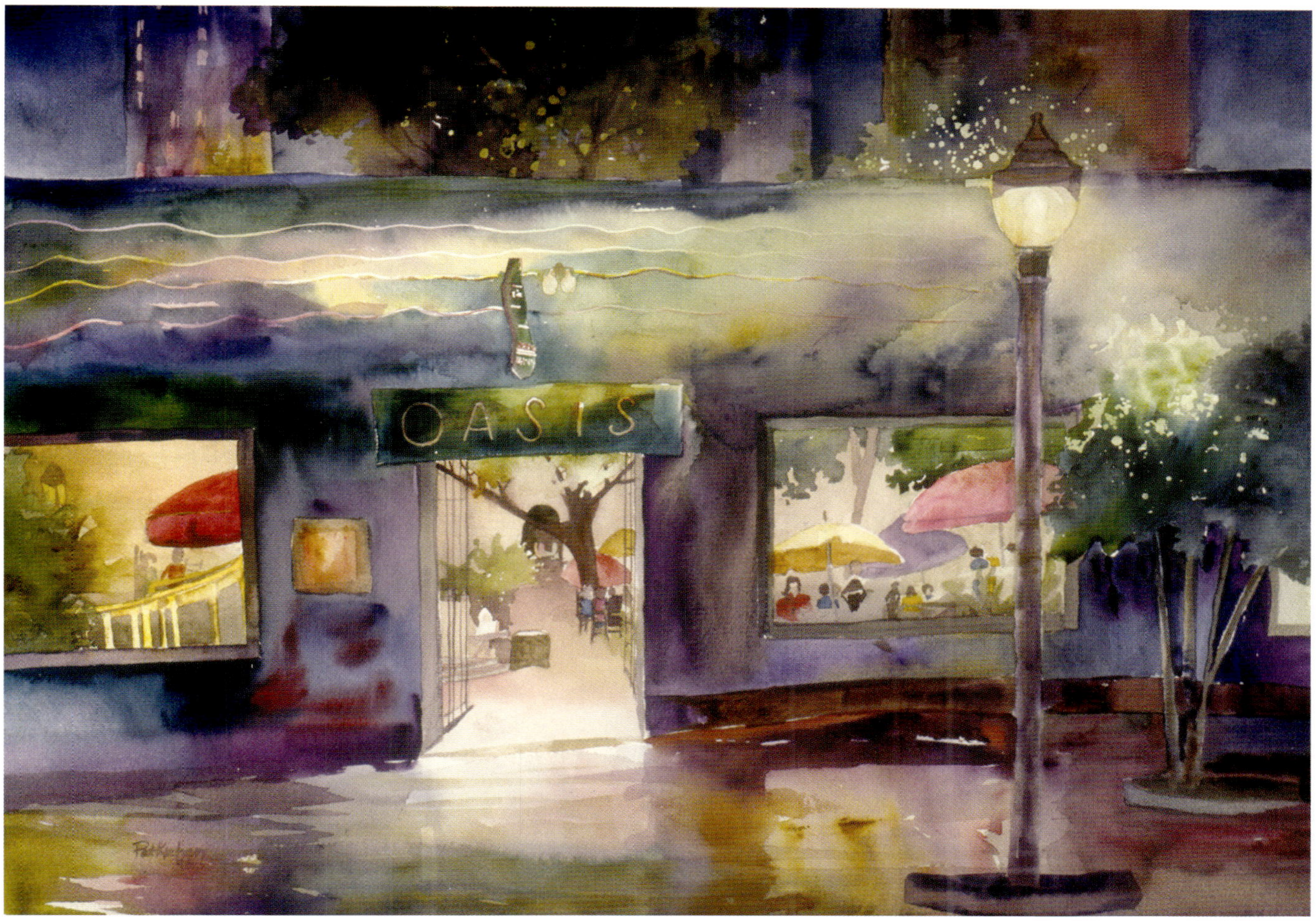

The West End: Oasis

watercolor
22x30

This is a restaurant in the West End, which is now under the name of Landry's Seafood Restaurant. The vantage point of the patio—an interesting vista of buildings, lights, and sky—fascinated me. It has quite an open feeling, with the Dallas skyline in the background. That is why I chose to paint the scene.

Old City Park

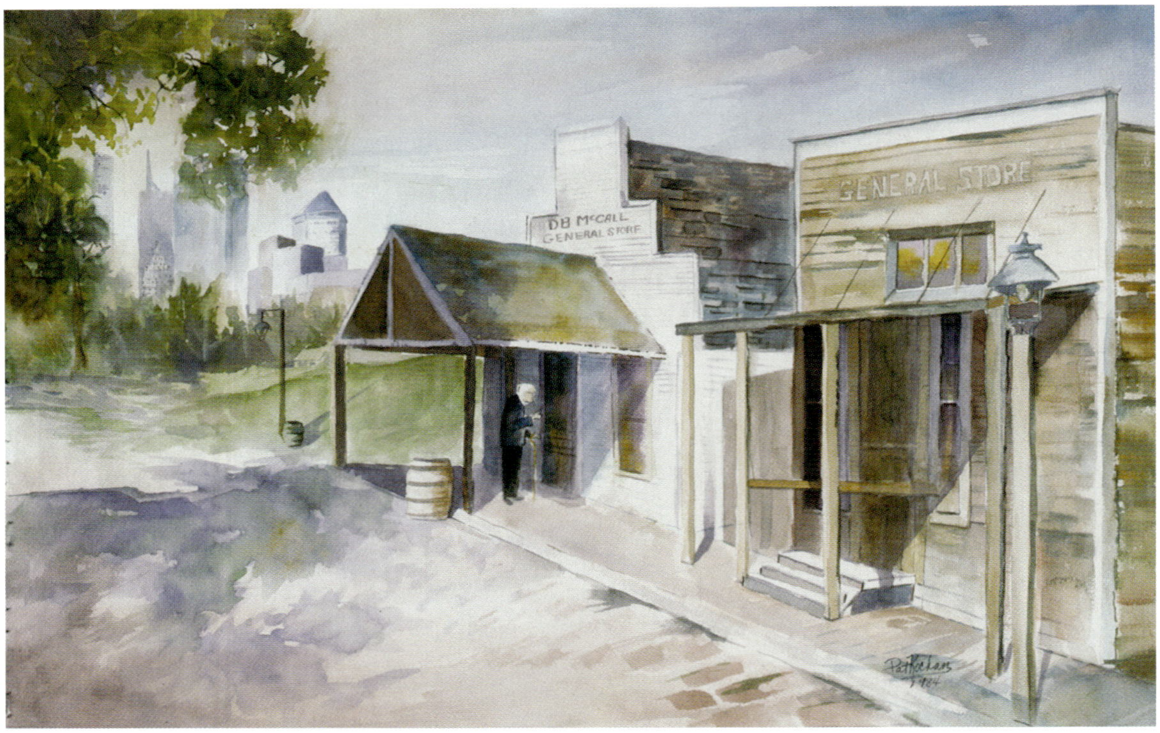

The Bank and General Store

watercolor
15x22

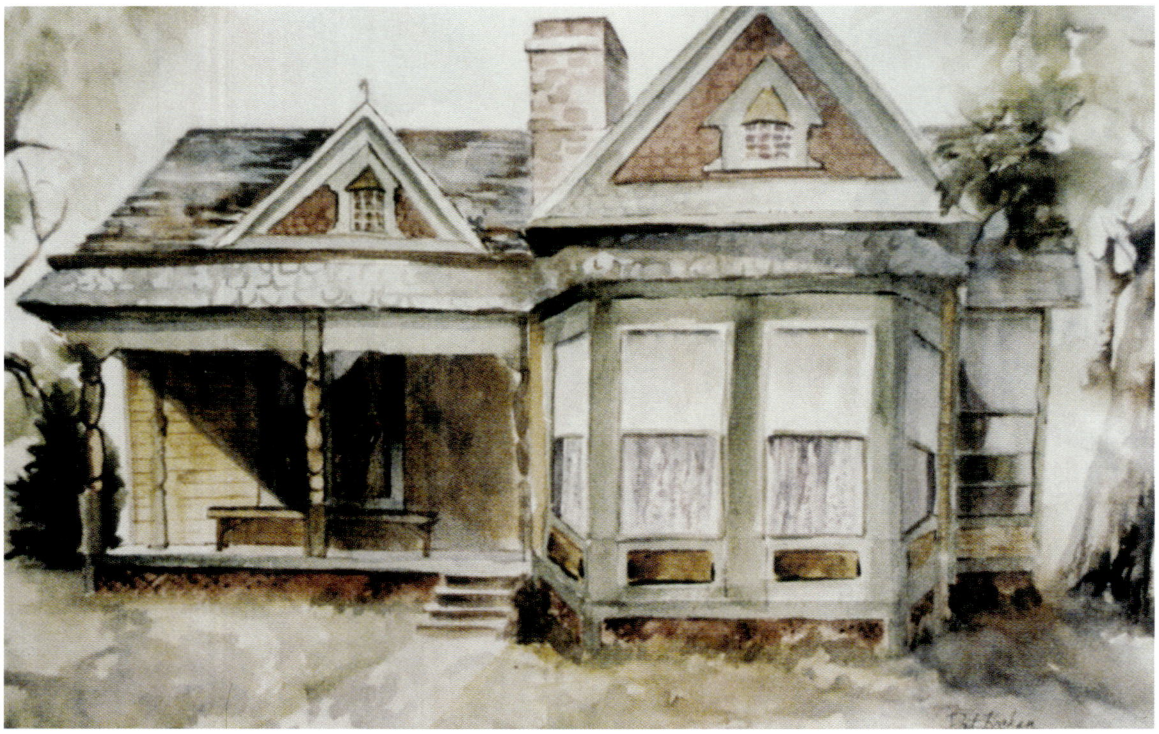

Doctor's House

watercolor
15x22

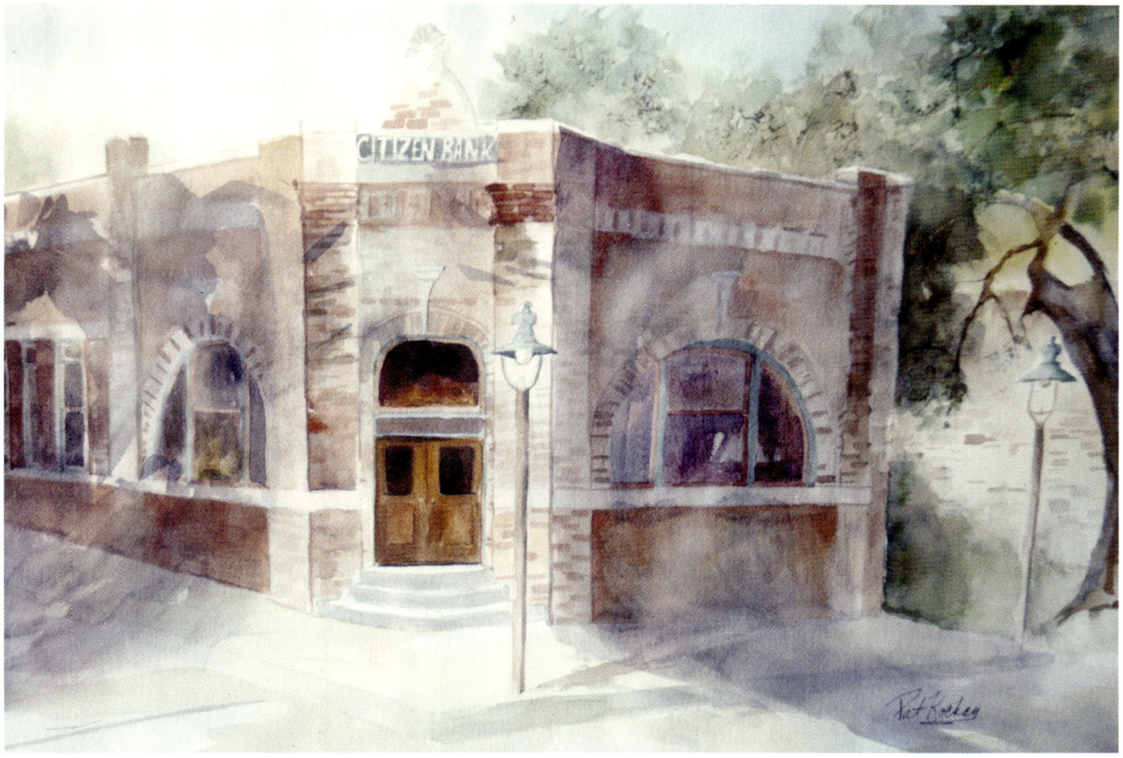

Bank

watercolor
16x20

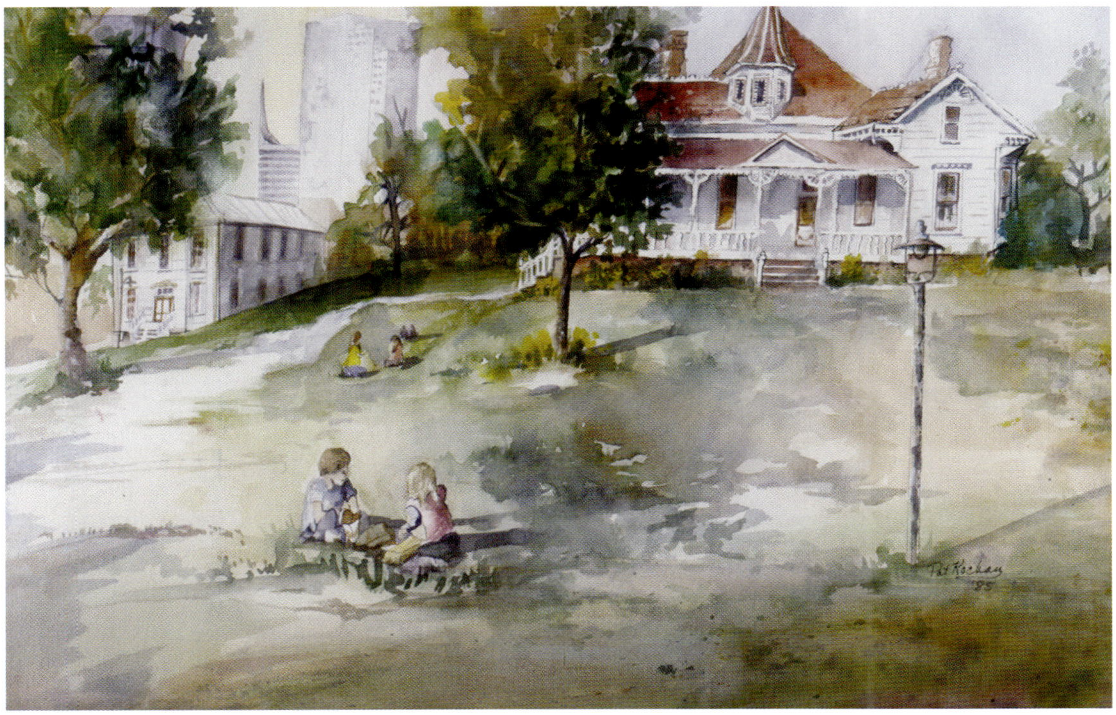

Picnic on the Lawn

watercolor
15x22

Belo Mansion

watercolor
22x30

I remember this building as a funeral home, where I attended my first funeral. I was six and very uncomfortable; Mom pinched me and told me to sit still. The building is really beautiful inside. In 2003, I was commissioned to paint a picture of the new pavilion at the Belo Mansion. Several other paintings of mine also hang there.

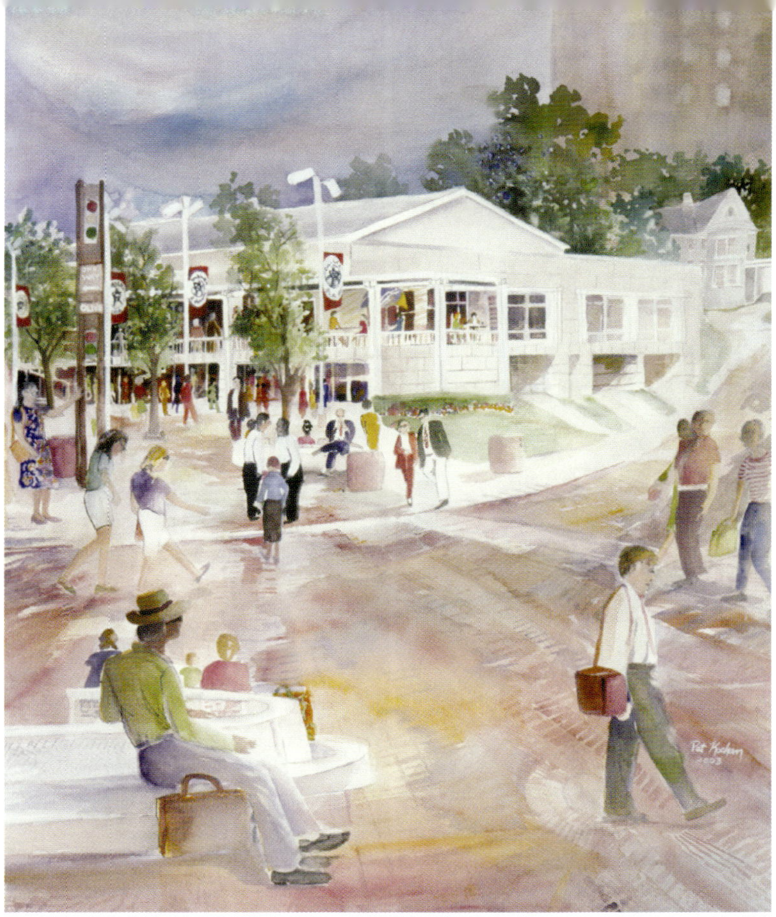

Pavilion at the Belo Mansion

watercolor
41x32

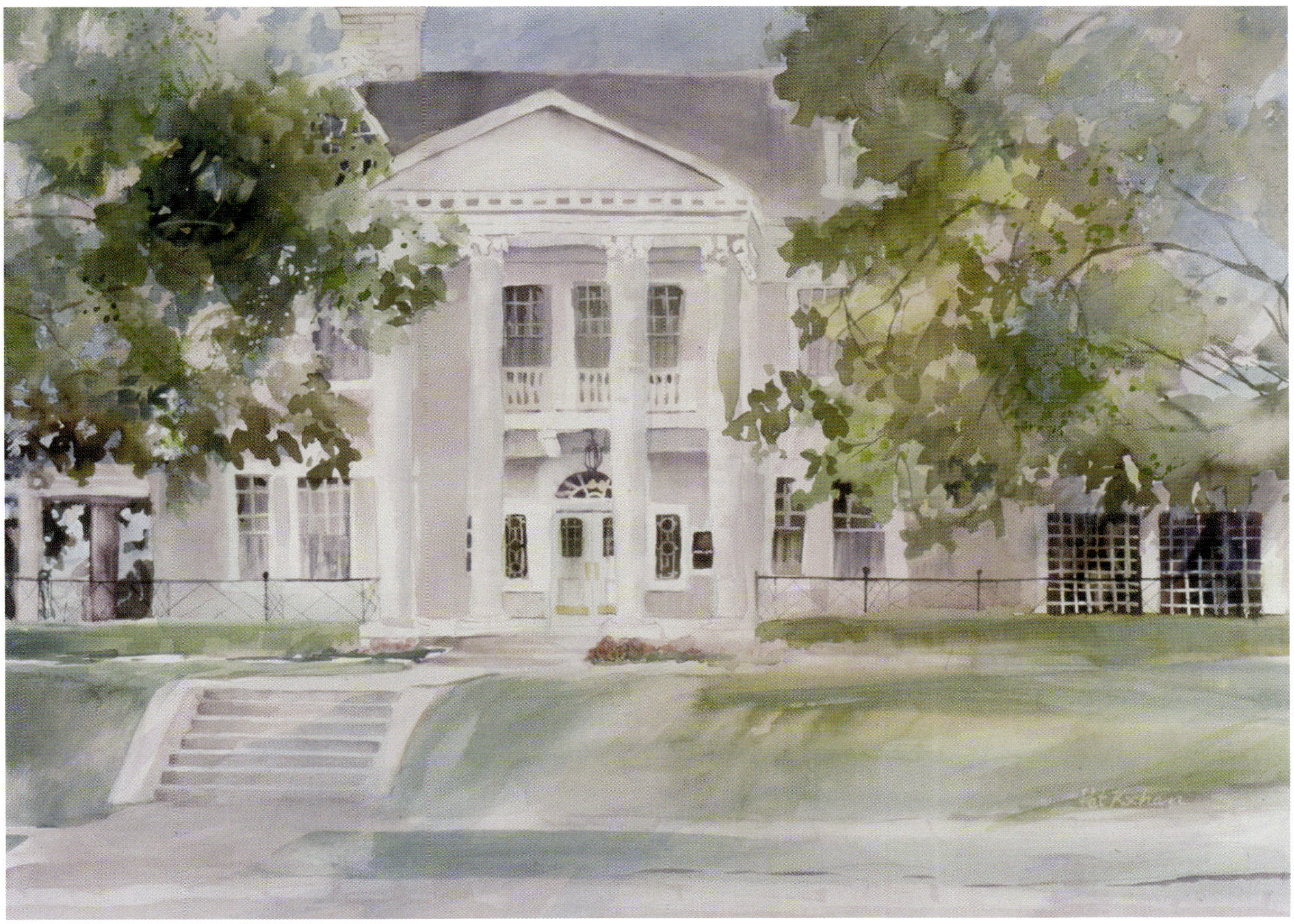

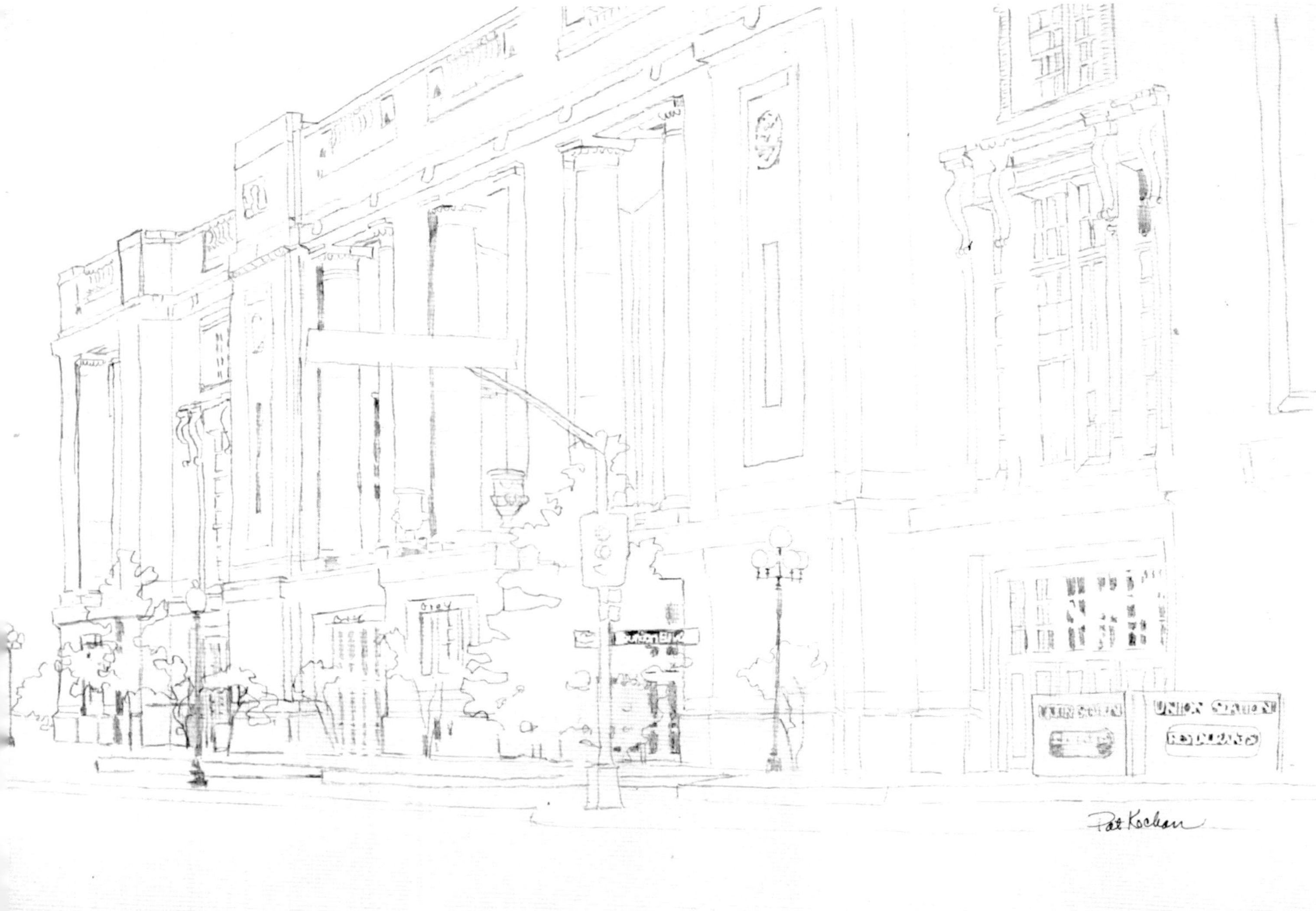

Union Station Sketch

drawing
22x30

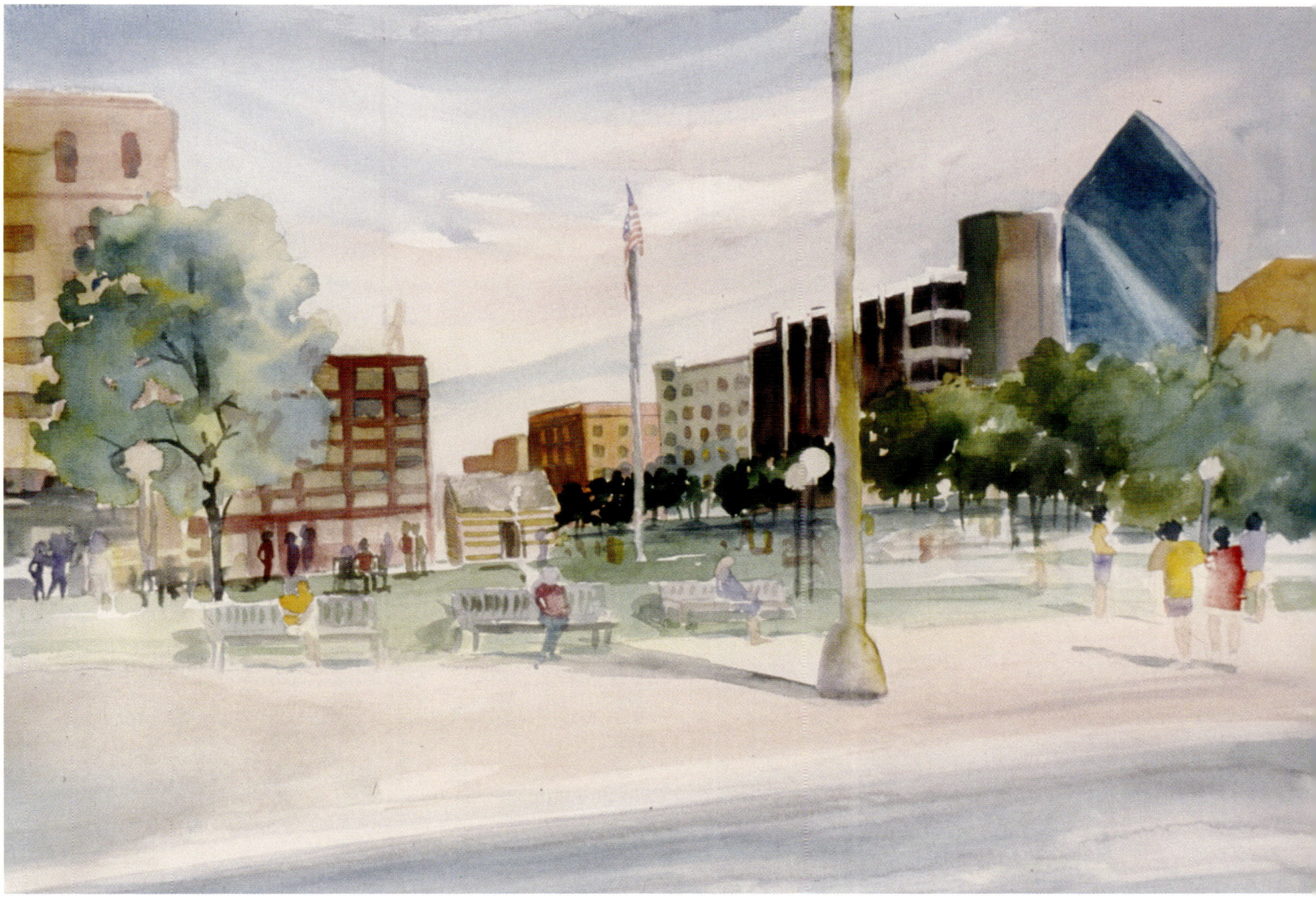

John Neely Bryan Cabin

watercolor
22x30

The Municipal Building Diptych

watercolor
22x30, 22x30

The extensive columns, arch windows, and ornate embellishments of the Municipal Building were a creative challenge for me to paint.

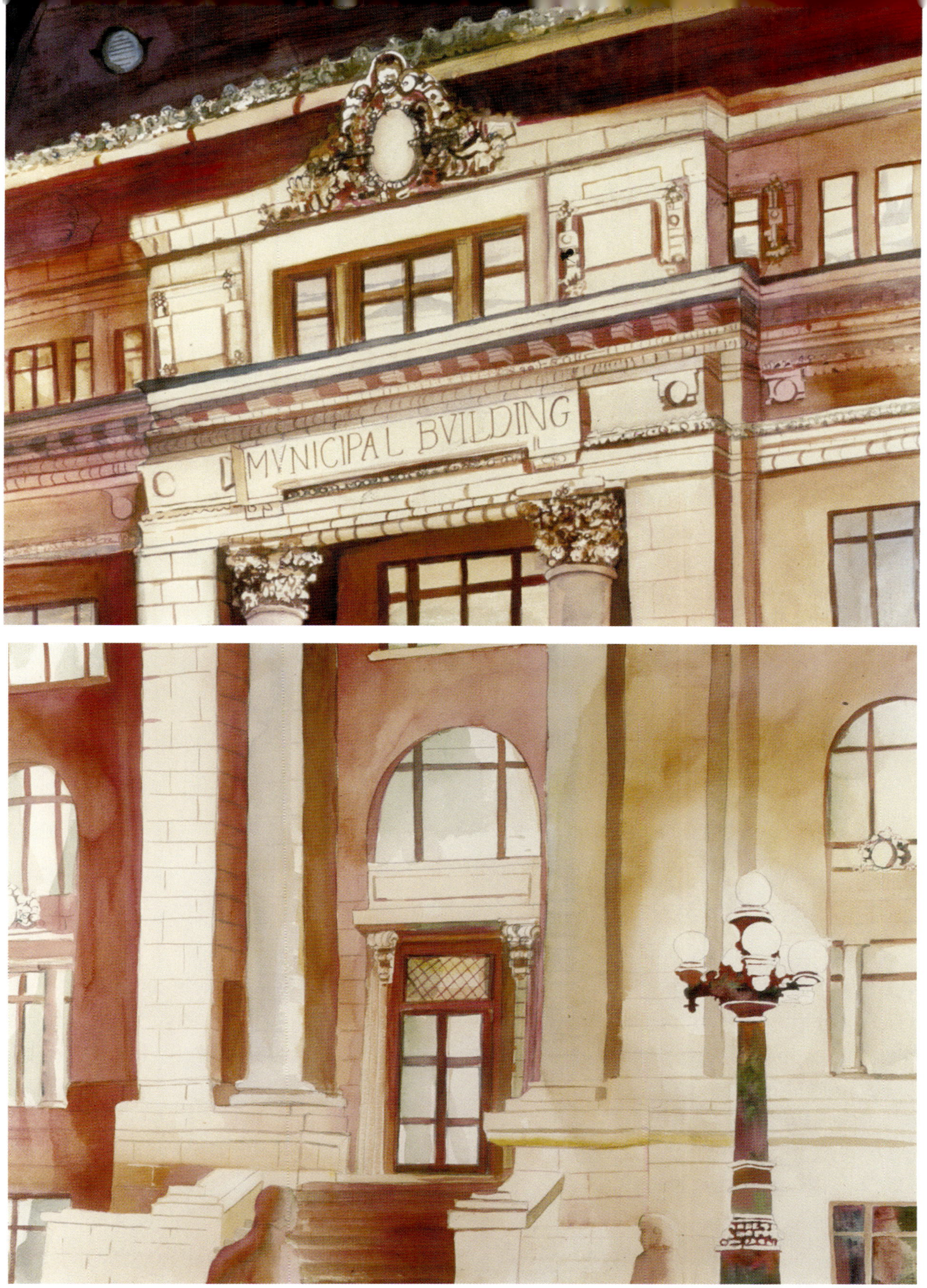
MVNICIPAL BVILDING

Who Was Involved?

watercolor/computer image of painting
30x22

The Dallas Schoolbook Depository, where Lee Harvey Oswald was said to have stood when he shot John F. Kennedy in November 1963, was later turned into a historical museum about the shooting. I wasn't interested in taking the museum tour when it opened. As a Dallas native, I had lived through the happenings, the media reports, and the anguish of the actual events as this horrible piece of history was being made here in my hometown.

While creating this downtown series of paintings, I knew I must include a painting about this event, so, I painted the view I imagined Oswald would have from that window on the sixth floor. The figure represents Oswald. The date is evident on the wall. On the far right is the Adolphus Hotel, viewed from the window of the bar. The bar was owned at that time by Jack Ruby who, in the course of events, shot and killed Oswald. That right-hand piece is a collaged computer image from one of my previous paintings of the Adolphus Hotel.

A few years ago my daughter asked me to go with her to visit the Sixth Floor Museum. I was shocked when I saw it for the first time. It looked just like the painting I had conceived in my mind, with the exception of the many boxes present on the sixth floor site but missing from the painting.

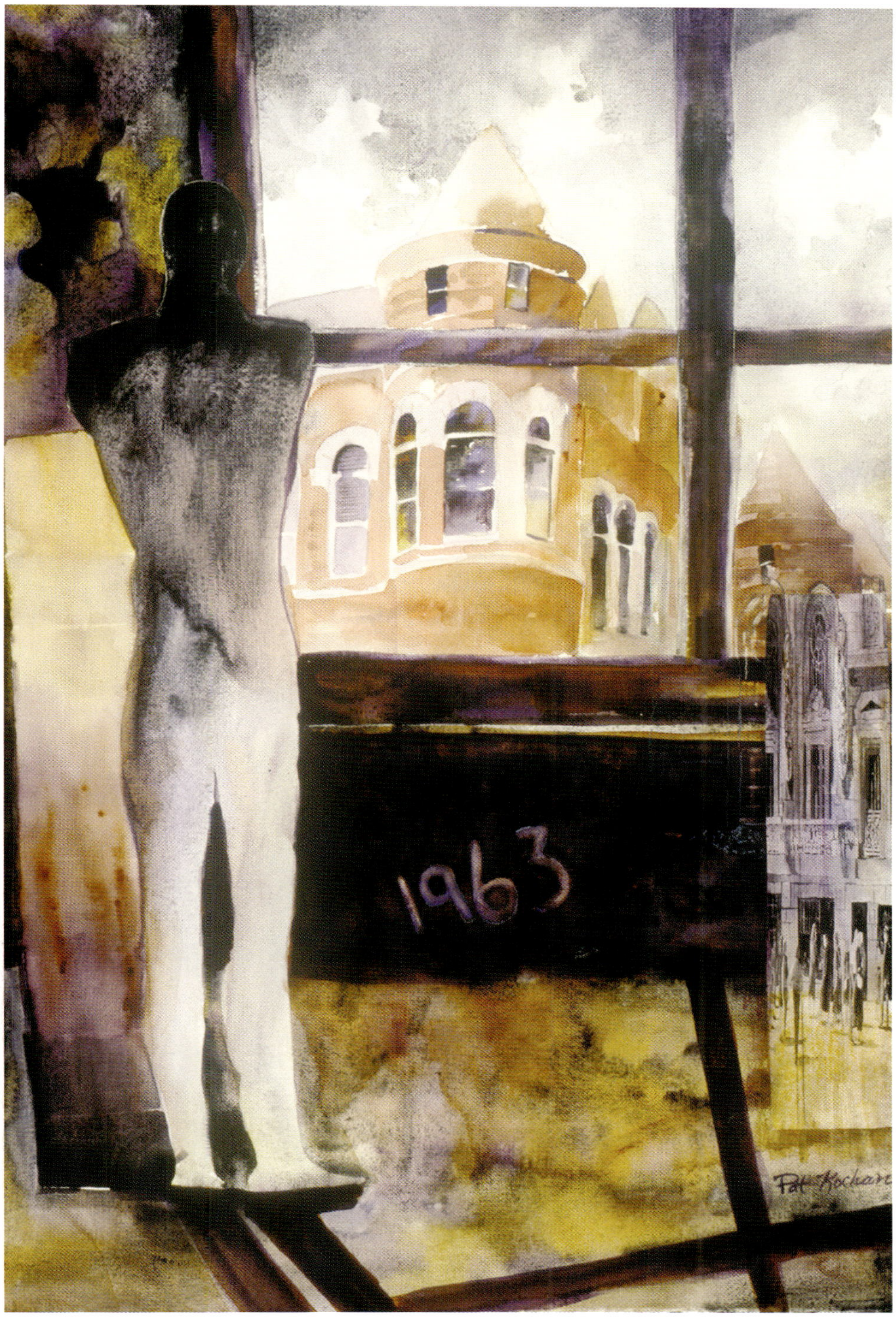
1963
Pat Kochan

Dallas Courthouse

watercolor/gouache
22x30

Many people refer to the Victorian-style Dallas County Courthouse as “Big Red.” In 1999, it was converted into a museum so that all may enjoy its wonderful history.

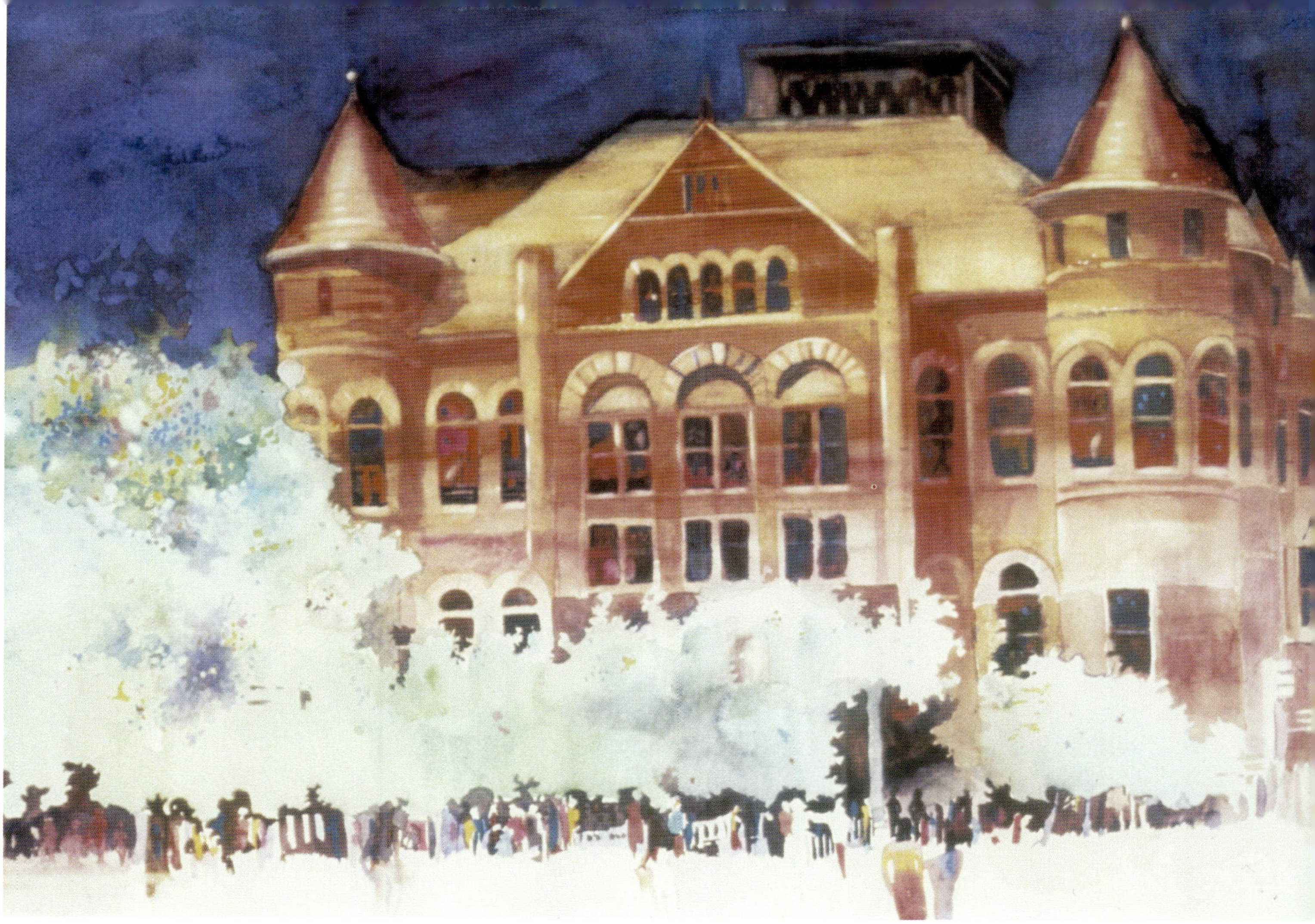

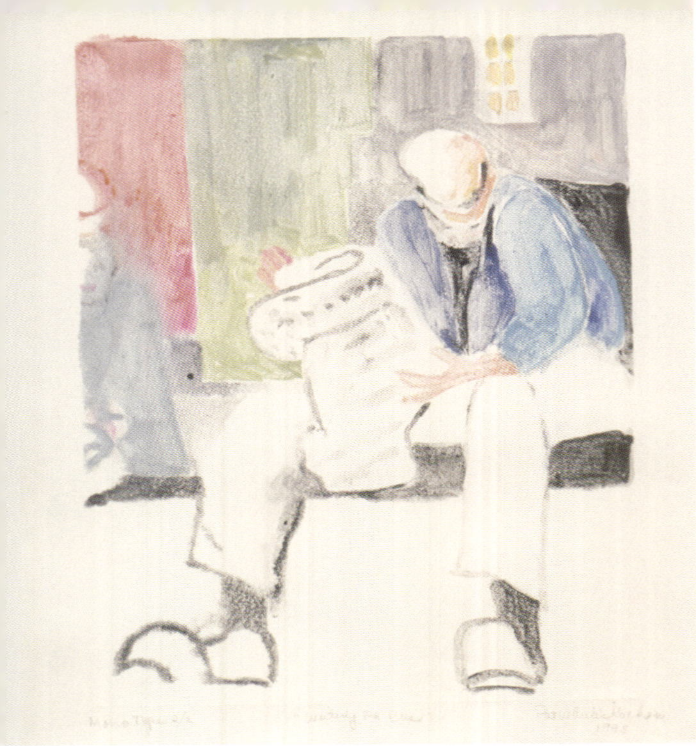

Waiting for a Bus

monotype
15x11

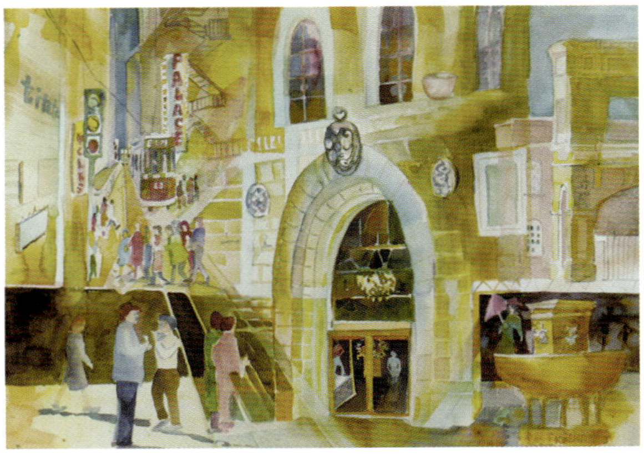

Dallas Relics

watercolor
22x30

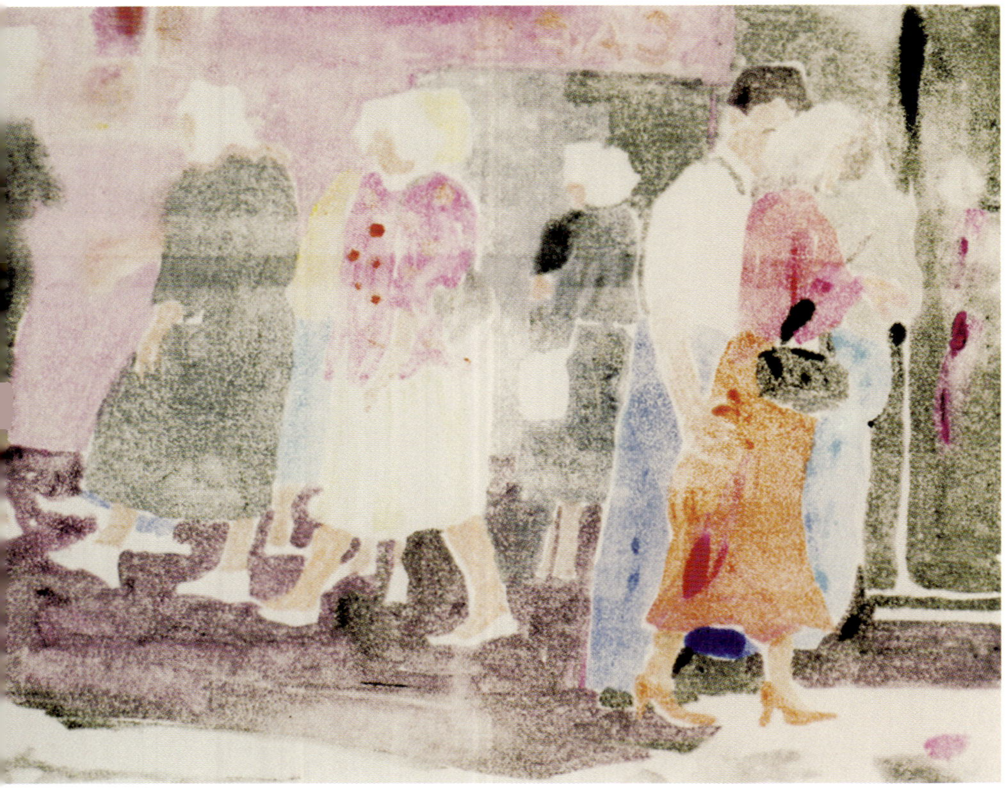

Lunch Hour

monotype
11x15

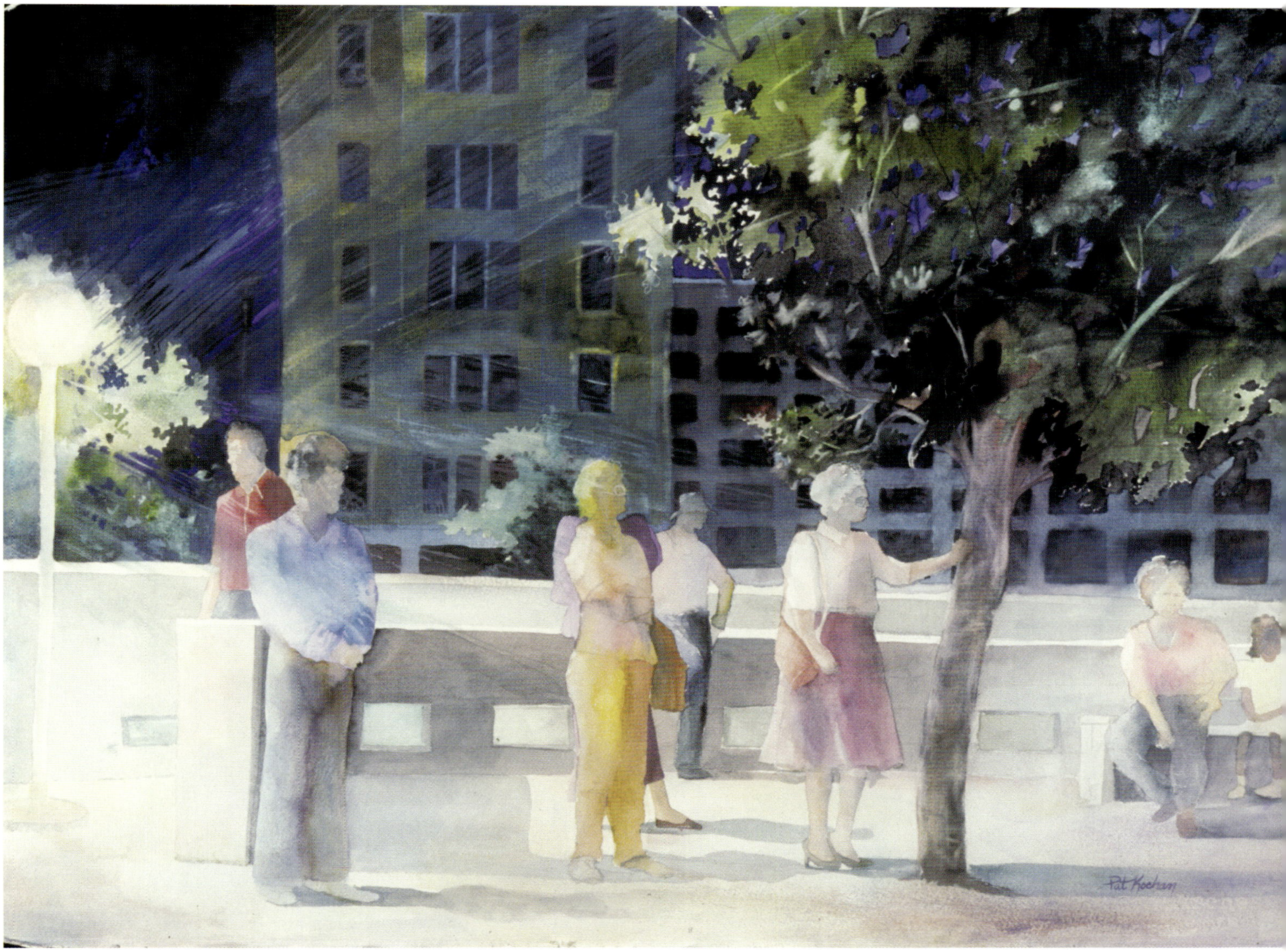

Bus Stop II

watercolor
22x30

I was intrigued by people waiting for a bus, in particular by how they ignored each other. This is near One Main Place, from the Bus Stop series.

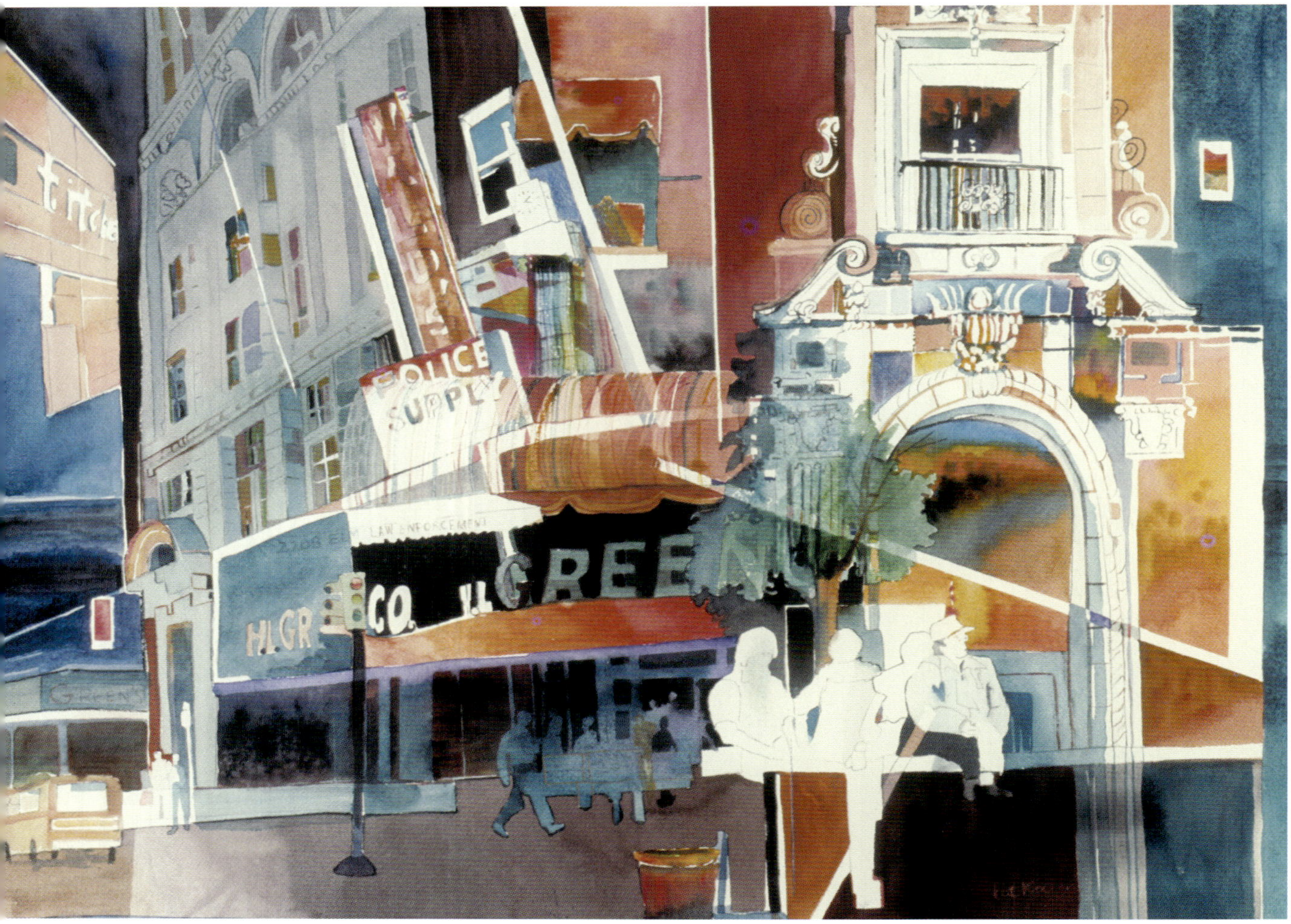

Parts of Dallas

watercolor
22x30

This is a montage of buildings in downtown Dallas: Titches-Goettinger Department Store, H. L. Green Co., Wald's, and the Dallas Plaza Hotel.

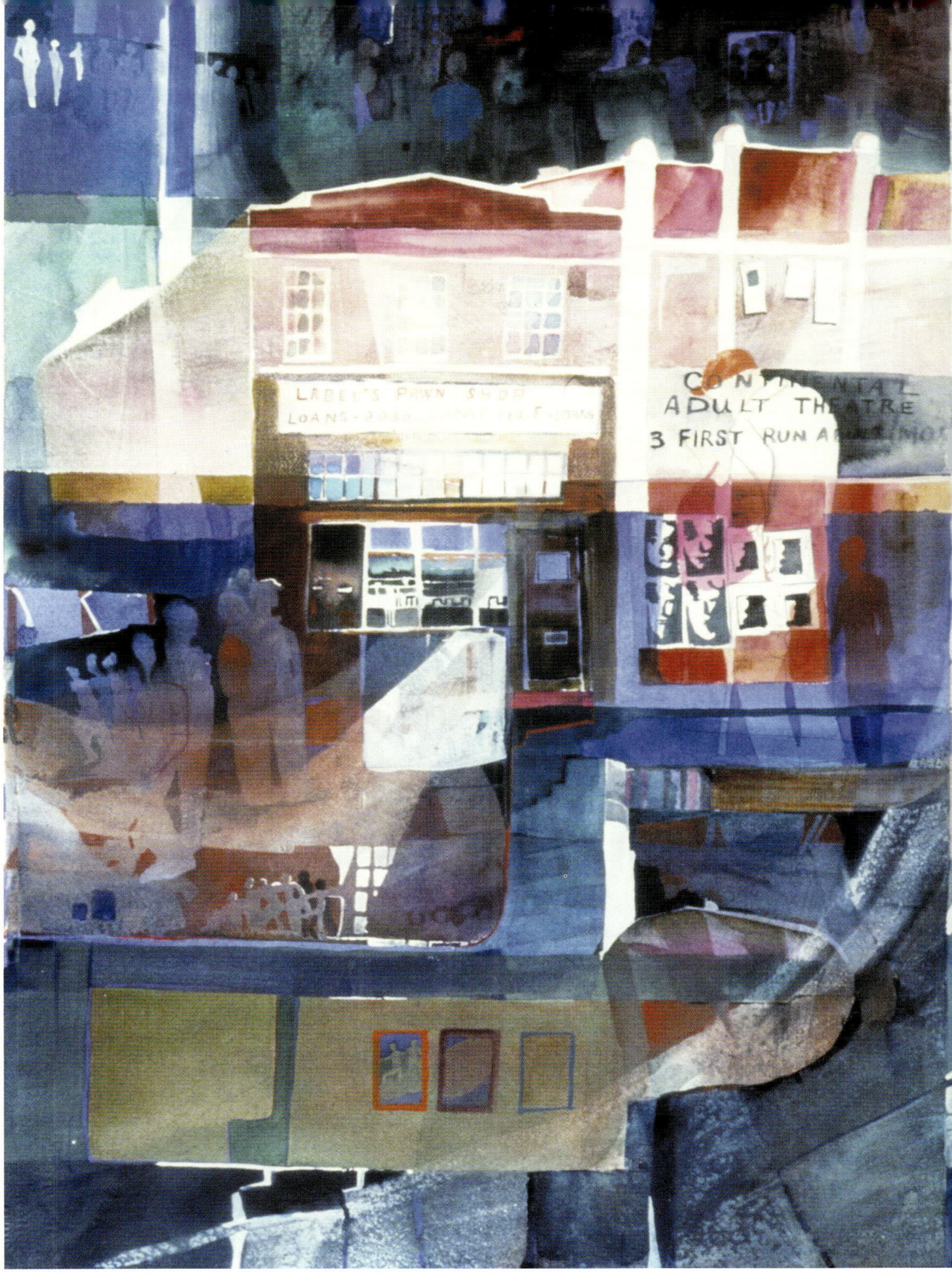

Road of Life Series: End of the Road

watercolor/gouache
30x22

These buildings were at the corner of Elm Street and Central Expressway. A pawnshop and an empty building covered with pasted pictures, advertisements, and graffiti are shown. The beggar, who I have used in several paintings, represents the end of the road and maybe a street person's last bit of hope.

Majestic at Night III was displayed in the mayor's conference room at City Hall in 1991 for a one-year period. The people of Dallas will always be grateful to Mayor Annette Strauss for her unending support of the arts and local artists.

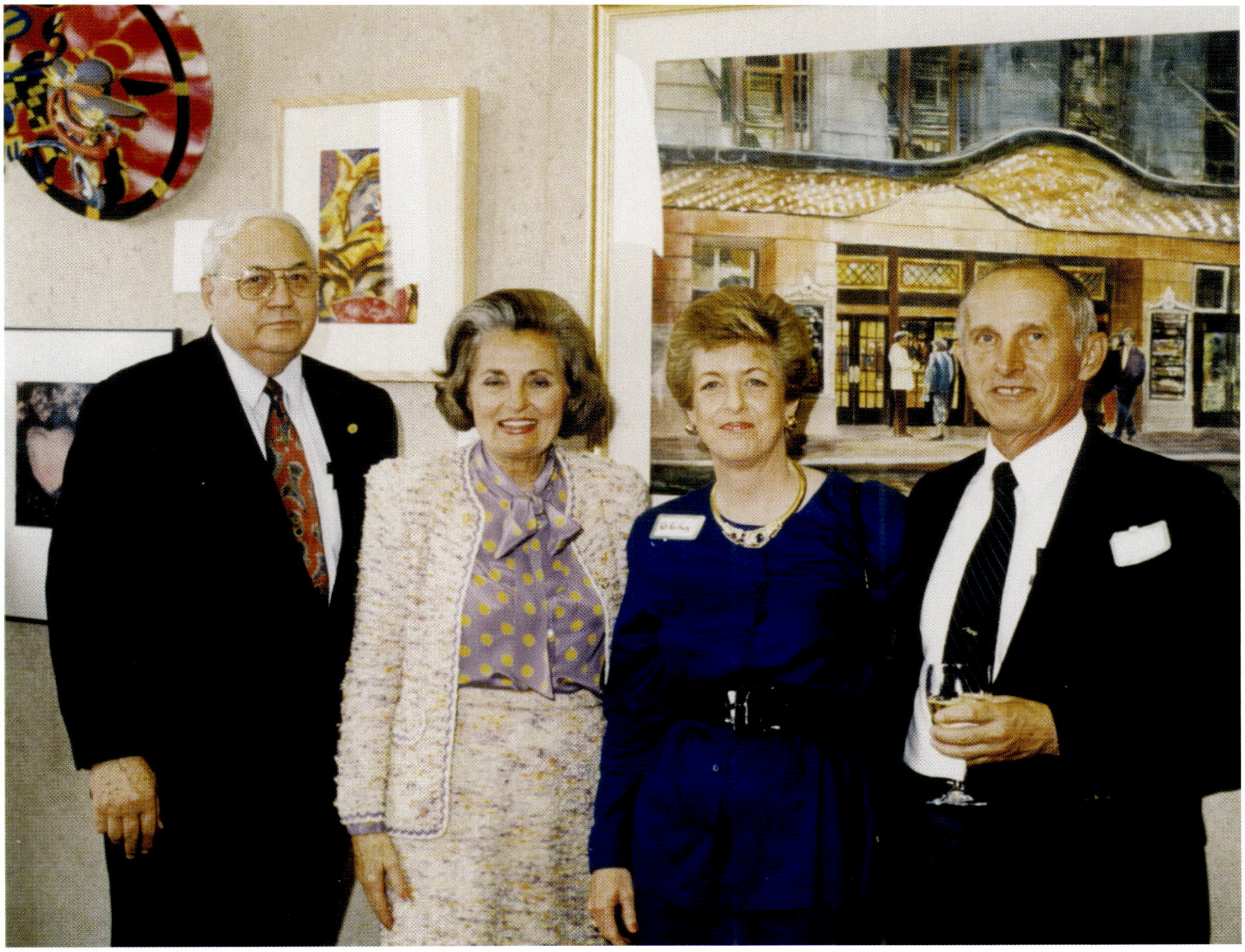

Pictured from left to right: City Manager Richard Knight, Mayor Annette Strauss, and Pat and John Kochan.

INDEX

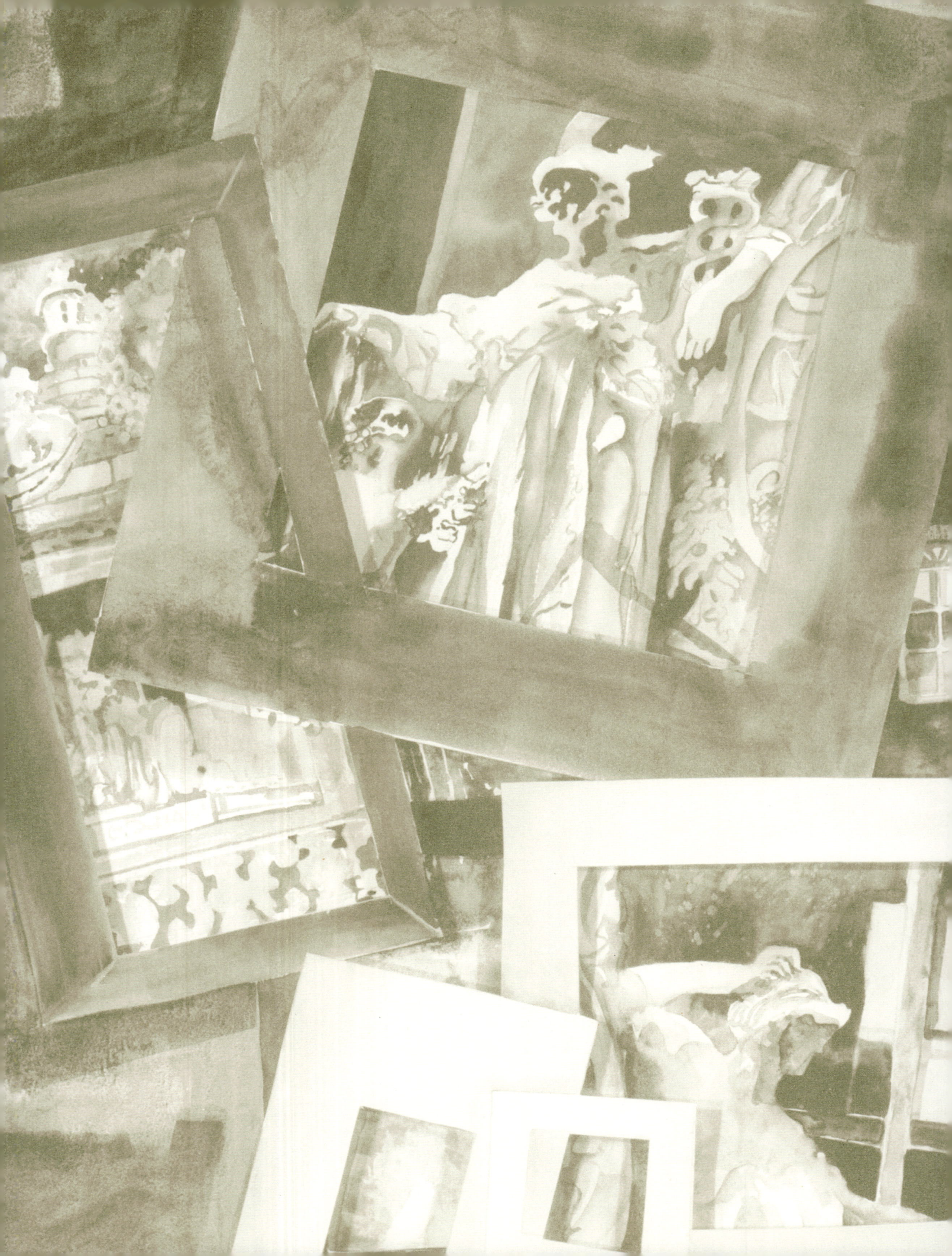